When Crows Call

IHSAN JONES

Copyright © 2012 Ihsan Jones

All rights reserved.

ISBN:978-0-615-72401-0
ISBN-13:0615724019

DEDICATION

This book is dedicated to my children and grandchildren, so they will never forget that in my heart…I carry a gift.

CONTENTS

	Introduction-Signs	i
1	Dreams Do Come True	1
2	When Crows Call	Pg #23
3	They Come Back	Pg #42
4	Exploring Dreams	Pg #50
5	Letter To Oprah	Pg #61
6	Passing The Gift	Pg #119
7	It's Hard To Know What The Future Holds…	Pg #134

Introduction

Signs:

It Wasn't An Accident

-When the bird pecked the lady.

-When The Crows lined up on the telephone wire above my parents house.

-When I saw the silhouette of my son in law on the stairs and then...

-When the Lone Crow showed up in Germany

-When my Granddaughter had the dream instead of me

-When I was in the store shopping and knew from the radio that the person dead was someone close.

-When I was drawn to the hospital where I had last seen my Father

-When my relatives die they come back to tell me something.

-When we were drawn to a particular park that appeared out of nowhere.

-When I had the dreams the nights before and then saw the figure.

-When I was questioning God and all there was about life and was drawn to scripture.

CHAPTER ONE

DREAMS DO COME TRUE

I awoke with death staring me in the face. It was a dark shadowy figure confronting me – standing over me. My face had been covered by a hand and perhaps some sort of plastic sheet. The figure withdrew its hand but not the plastic covering. I attempted to take a deep breath. My mouth again sucked in the plastic sheet but I managed a fairly good breath through my nostrils.

As my mind cleared from the confusion of sleep it became clear that the hand had been trying to smother me. If I had not awakened when I did, I would have most certainly been dead.

My eyes met a strange and unfamiliar world. It presented a strange combination of my own room, darkened, and things I could not recognize. I could see the whole picture as clear as day but still, I could not understand it. Presently, the figure moved away swiftly. I heard voices. They were discussing me as if I were a rare, unique specimen of some kind.

Trying to get a handle on what was taking place, I lay there looking up, my eyes looking left and right. The others towered over me, peering down. From time to time they huddled together and chattered. I could not make out most of what they were saying. One phrase came through to me, however.

"Should we take her?"

Perhaps that voice was familiar but I couldn't be sure. The other voices sounded familiar but through their low, almost confidential tone, I could not make out what they were saying.

I continued to gasp for a breath even though the covering had disappeared from my mouth moments before. I had obviously been deprived of air for some time.

Could this be real or something from a fantasy? It was the stuff of dreams and yet I seemed to be awake. I could still see the other world present before me. I could still hear the voices. As they hovered above me one face melded into the others. Were these my saviors from the one that had covered my face or were they his cohorts – in league together for some unimaginable undertaking?

There were familiar voices – perhaps my aunts and uncles, maybe even my parents – but I could not attach voices to bodies or faces.

Again, I heard the question.

"Should we take her?"

Again, I could not make out the source or any response.

I did not move. It may have been because I was sapped of energy. It may have been that I was being held there on the table. One thing I did understand. I was laying there like a specimen being scrutinized as I found myself drifting between the known and the unknown.

Another world was definitely present. Had I been taken to it or had it come and invaded mine? I hadn't the faintest idea what it was. Who the beings were baffled me – strange shapes and yet familiar voices. None of it made sense and yet there it was – there I was – both clear as could be. The shadow, of which I had first become aware, stood off to the side at that point, nothing more than a large silhouette being lifted away and fading off to the side into the shadows. My vision could not penetrate that darkness – it was an area of deep nothingness.

I concentrated on what I could see. There was a beam of light that played off the white walls, dimly illuminating parts of the room. There was an opening leading to some sort of pathway. It may have been from where the voices were coming – those familiar voices I had heard that were disassociated from bodies and faces.

It was not really a clear message – more of a nebulous impression. It seemed to have to do with something about if I stared long enough and kept asking more questions I could join them. Why would I want to join them? It was all quite confusing. They may have been inviting me to come and see without being seen or heard. It was something I sensed without really understanding. I was to follow the path if the answer had been 'yes.' I assumed that was the answer to the question about whether or not I should be 'taken', although what 'taken' referred to I had no idea. There was something about I couldn't be taken alive. Death apparently was the precursor for what I would seek – following the path. I lay still, silently in awe of the fully incomprehensible experience.

The shadows passed and the voices faded. My world brightened and more familiar sounds returned. Before long I could only see the whiteness. Through my gradually clearing mental fog, I came to recognize that it was the whiteness of my television screen. There were the sounds of the humming refrigerator and an occasional chirp from the power challenged smoke detector in the ceiling above.

I remembered having muted the television before I fell asleep. My mind raced – so many things to remember and so many questions to ask and answer. My eyes scanned the room. There was a comforting calmness about the situation. My heart thumped hard as every memory, every thought, flashed through my head. My eyes opened wide to see every detail. If one of those beings had been present, or, in fact, if anything had even moved, I have no doubt that I would have had heart failure.

I soon discovered that I was there alone. Gradually my breathing returned to normal. It had been the first time since the scenario had begun that I could gather my thoughts with any sense of certainty. My mind was drawn to scripture. There were two bibles sitting atop the refrigerator. Something kept telling me that the answers I sought were in them. Like so many times before, I let that thought slide. I didn't pick up the bibles. But something was not done. Over and over it called out to me to read them.

I silenced the voices and attempted to realign myself in the contour of the couch. I had been sleeping in an awkward position. I had been lying on my back and felt vulnerable. Normally, I wouldn't sleep that way but the night before I had been reclining there contemplating important questions. I had fallen asleep disappointed that I had not found any answers. I had been talking with God, asking questions that had become very important to me.

"Why do we exist?"

"Why are there other beings?"

"What is the significance of life and the universe?"

"What ultimately does God want us to do?"

And most importantly, "Why did he make us?"

I approached that discussion with neutrality, giving God no he or she connotation. I sought clarity about life and all its complexities. I asked the simple question and was given a simple response.

"You have to be taken somewhere else to be shown the answer, but once the truth is discovered, you cannot 'live' to talk about it."

It took many days for me to figure that out.

A week or so prior to all of this, I had another dream. Like many dreams, it wasn't specific but showed one of my sons in some sort of distress. I hadn't felt death in that dream but there was an uneasiness and disturbance that stayed with me afterward. Like most dreams that felt so important, I had to inquire. To inquire meant to check on everyone near and dear to me.

"Are you ok?" I asked as I made the phone calls.

I was unable to reach my son. It was he that I was most concerned about. I reached out to my daughters for solace and their thoughts about the meaning of the dream.

"Maybe everything will be okay," my youngest daughter said. "Not being able to find him is not unusual. Maybe he'll get back to you in a few days."

And he did. So, I had peace for the moment.

Still, I did have the dream and the memory of it continued to intrude into my thoughts. It became a set of constant, though nebulous, feelings and images. Panic set in. I began to worry that maybe it was something else – somebody else – and not him that had been the true focus of that dream. The images began to clear. It was his face that accompanied those memories.

Sometimes my dreams treated me that way. They took me off path, establishing a growing sense of anxiety that catapulted my thoughts into the unknown and just left them hanging there. I had no recourse – no positive action that I could take. I waited as time stood still ,understanding that some chilling climax would eventually show itself.

That most recent dream was different in form. It had come over me in my waking moment. That was unsettling to me.

Time passed.

Anxiety built.

My unsettled nature became apparent to others.

By then, all my children had become privy to the conversation. That thrust them into the game of wait and see right along with me. Past experiences had forged one truth for them: If their mother tells them she had a dream, they should listen. My dreams always come true in some shape or fashion, especially the disturbing ones. Those are the ones that provide meaning to life and death. They usually involve someone close to my heart like a family member.

I often feel like a link in a chain. When that link is pulled I can feel it tighten and strain. Sometimes the chain is yanked so hard a link is broken. Those are the times during which I have my most intense – often distressing – dreams.

After checking with everyone and praying that my mental mist would clear, the feelings would usually retreat – leave. This time it hung on, telling me my work with it was not finished. Something was still to take place. I could not see what. There was never any turning back the clock on what I had already felt but the experiences often settled into the recesses of my mind, there to recall, but, not forcing themselves into my consciousness. The underlying themes, however, reliably played out. If I dreamed of death, then death was imminent. If I dreamed of sickness then something or someone was in distress. That was a fact of my existence.

I concluded that the shadow in that last, wakeful dream, cautioned me to be careful about what I asked for because, although I might get it, it would not necessarily be in the form I might desire or even suspect.

It was one thing to tell my children about the contents of the last dream but quite another thing to try and explain that it came to me while I was awake. I struggled with how I could present it to them. How could I possibly put into words what I saw and make them understand? They would have to believe that their mother had seen though a veil into another world and still believe that she had not lost her senses.

I could never really tell how much of it they bought when I shared my dreams with them. I understood if they didn't fully believe, but they were always cordial and supportive. I struggled with that myself. I always had the need to tell someone. Early in my life, my mother had been my patient and compassionate confidant. She is long gone so, now, I only have my children to rely on. I wouldn't dare trust another soul with the knowledge of this gift I have. My children are my life. I must help them understand all that I understand about it. It may well blossom within them some day.

I had surgery pending. The date was set and I was making the rounds of all my pre-surgery appointments. There was a surreal element that encompassed it from the moment I had met the doctor. My hip was hurting and I walked with a limp – those things were real. The fact that the medical people believed that my condition would require surgery to correct also seemed real. Somewhere deep inside me, however, I had lingering doubts – an uneasiness – about the surgery.

All of that was taking place in and around the times of these two dreams. I had all but dismissed the first one after talking with my son. My first doctor had explained my condition to me and assured me that surgery was indicated and that she had no reason to believe the outcome would not be completely successful – no more pain – no more limping.

My x-rays were transferred to the surgeon – an orthopedic specialist. I overheard the conversation between him and my doctor. The specialist's quick survey of my chart and test results seemed to confirm to him what I had been told.

"This lady needs to be taken care of right away as her arthritis is severe and her condition is degenerating."

It had been his comment to my doctor in the next room. I overheard through the cracked door. He reentered the room and delivered his verdict – surgery and soon. He said his colleague would be the best one to perform it because he was younger and more up to date on the specialized procedures the operation would require. I left the office grateful and thankful that day. Thankful that my primary doctor took time enough to recognize my condition and order follow-up. I had seen two other doctors prior to her who brushed me off as merely being overweight.

"Lose thirty pounds and your condition will right itself," I was told.

Neither one of them took time to examine my history and other elements related to my health to determine what my ailments really were. This doctor had taken the time and that meant a lot to me.

A series of appointments had been scheduled. They involved more x-rays, ultrasound testing, EKG's, and blood work. I also met with another doctor for general medical clearance – to make certain my body was up to the surgery. The doctor seemed nice but really left no lasting impression on me. He tried to joke but I didn't catch most them. I choose to believe it was the nature of his humor rather my inability to get a joke that posed the problem, there.

Two weeks passed and the time for the surgery was at hand. I had been preparing mentally for that day although in many ways it seemed unbelievable that it was actually going to come about. My oldest son was coming to town to stay with me. He was in it for the long haul and was prepared to help me with cooking, cleaning, lifting, etc.

I saw the fourth doctor just before the surgery for one final check up. He was more memorable than my surgeon. Perhaps that was because of his accent or how he had difficulty pronouncing

English words. It may have been the off beat way he had of explaining my preparation for the surgery.

"Make sure you wash very good the night before – using soap and water and cleaning in places, well you know."

He made the motions. I put into words what he couldn't.

"You mean under my arms and in all my crevices don't you?"

"Yes." He nodded.

How elementary, I thought to myself. Why would a doctor think one would not take a bath before having something as important as surgery? I left his office with less than a fully positive view of him. Funny how things work however, because he turned out to be my biggest advocate.

My son had arrived the day before the surgery. As he came the door I was leaving. There was only time to exchange kisses. I had promised my youngest daughter that I would attend her baby's christening. My son's late arrival left him tired so I convinced him to rest and took a daughter with me.

The service was held at the house of the great grandparents on the paternal side. I was used to having such rites held in a church. I sat through the ceremony with an open mind because after all church is church regardless whether it is at someone's house or in a fancy building. This was a small, comfortable, family affair and conveyed an atmosphere of love and caring.

I felt joyful and was immediately caught up in the spirit of their praying and singing. Her parents had dressed my new grandbaby in a lovely christening frock. Everyone took pictures. Afterward there was lots of food. Her other grandma had made a special cake. It had met with disaster as somebody had dropped it, however nobody seemed to mind. Most of it was salvaged and every crumb was enjoyed.

It was a very nice time and I was glad I had attended. The grandparents seemed like fine people and I enjoyed chatting with them. The night before I was so tired I wasn't sure I would be able to go so it had become a last minute decision.

I mentioned my dreams to my daughter – the baby's mother. I told her that I had been drawn toward scripture because of it. It was not because I felt I needed to go to church, because if ever there was a Godly person, it would be me. I just don't regularly attend in a formal sense. I mentioned to my daughter about the uneasy feeling that still accompanied the first dream – the one about my son. I later revealed to her about the second dream, the one I call the "waking" moment experience, because it happened after being asleep and in the middle of the night. I told her that I had felt like reading the bible right after that encounter and that it was as though something continued to urge me in that direction. I told her that the 'sneaking' shadow appeared to be trying to steal my breath from me. I told her I wasn't sure if the other voices I heard were aware of what it was doing. It seemed somehow like a separate event – as if an unseen thief in the night.

The paternal grandfather was a spiritual man and had been the head of the church before they chose to have it at home. I didn't question why they no longer attended the pretty little church with the white picket fence. My daughter offered an explanation saying only that there was a disagreement among the elders and grandma and grandpa chose to worship at home. It then became apparent that half of my son in law's clan were the members that made up the church. I estimated there were nearly two hundred in attendance.

An event happened while I was in the car riding with my son in law to their house one day. The baby was still small and I had been cooking for them in spite of my leg and hip. We had dropped off his cousin on the way and parked in front of his grandpa's house. The end of the world predictions by some preacher had been dominating the airwaves. The news reporters were all over the place with the story. It was all to take place the next day.

Grandpa was sitting on a bench talking on his cell phone easing the mind of one of the sheep in his flock. It was an elderly lady worried about what was going to happen.

As we pulled to a stop, Grandpa approached me as I was sitting in the car. He leaned down and spoke.

"Oh, I thought you were your daughter," he said.

She would have normally been sitting in that spot instead of me.

"How are you?" I said as I rolled the window down.

"Are you scared," he asked.

At first I thought he meant the surgery but realized he couldn't have been talking about that. I hadn't discussed it with him. I guess I looked puzzled because he offered more.

"About the end of day prediction."

"Oh, that. No, I'm not. If its time to go there's nothing we can do about it."

"He'll come like a thief in the night," the man said.

Thief in the night...thief in the night. How could he have known that I had the dream. He didn't, of course. That was the phrase I was looking for, however. The shadow had been sneaking, acting like a thief!

I Googled the term as soon as I got home but wasn't satisfied with what I read. I thought it must be a part of scripture so I opened the bible. I couldn't find the phrase.

Several days later my daughter texted me some bible passages from grandpa as I had mentioned to her that the phrase he said stood out to me.

I read the bible passages. They were dead on what I had been thinking. (Revelation 3:3; Peter 2 3:10; First Thessalonians 5:2; Matthew 24:43)

Remember, therefore, what you have received and heard; hold it fast, and repent. But if you do not wake up, I will come like a thief, and you will not know at what time I will come to you.

The Surgery

I slept poorly the night before the surgery – tossing and turning. At one point my son passed my room and glimpsed in.

"What's wrong ma, you worried?"

"I can't sleep," I said. "Something keeps telling me I'm not going to make it. It keeps saying I'm going to die. The word 'die' keeps sounding over and over in my head to the point where I can't close my eyes."

"Wow," he said. "Well, maybe you shouldn't go through with it."

I dismissed the thought and slept lightly, off and on, until it was time to get up. I was to be there at 7 am. My daughter took me and my son was to join me later. They would all be there for the surgery. I got checked in. The nurse took the vitals and had me sign the paperwork. I kept wondering to myself, am I really here, is this really happening?

I figured the orthopedic doctor would be there early to talk with me one last time before surgery. The nurses did a good job of explaining how things were going to be. The entire staff treated me well. Even so, I don't remember any of them - their faces. Their voices, were surreal. I was put on a gurney and taken to the area where surgery was to take place. On the way, I had time to contemplate my situation. The sedatives had begun to take effect. The man in the white outfit that was pushing my bed was behind me and I couldn't see his face.

I was moving between white walls. There were bright lights overhead and a few windows. It was quiet and generally peaceful. In some way it all seemed familiar – like I had been there before, as if I had done all that before. *Deja vu* is the phrase that describes what I was feeling.

I continued down the hallway until we reached the elevator. The elevator took us to another floor. I was rolled into a hallway outside the operating room and greeted by another nurse. She explained about numbing me and the epidural I would receive. I told her that I was no stranger to hospitals or needles, having had several kids. I didn't look forward to having her stick a needle or tube in the middle of my back however.

The doctor stopped by just long enough to tell me I would have a new hip when I woke up. After that everything became a blur. The last thing I remember was being moved onto the operating table.

Several hours later the cobwebs began to clear. I could make out a shadowy figure standing over me and leaning down toward my face. "She's awake", I heard a woman's voice announce.

The shadowy figure leaned in closer and then coddled my

hand. The face gradually became clearer. It was the doctor. He spoke to me. All I heard was, "I'm sorry. I couldn't do the surgery."

I was waiting for the punch line since this man was known for his jokes.

"You're kidding right?" I managed.

The doctor mumbled things to me.

"I could have done the surgery, but I didn't want to butcher you. It required multiple cuts and I didn't want to mutilate you."

I was stunned. I wanted more of an answer than that.

"But doctor I pleaded. I eat organic. I eat healthy. I want to lose weight but I just can't exercise with this leg."

He looked at me over his shoulder as he walked away. Clearly the conversation was over. The room was all but cleared out except for two assistants with their back to me. I was still only half awake. Fading in and out I closed my eyes in disappointment.

Sometime later, I woke up back in the hospital room. There were cuffs around my legs. The nurse said they were providing electrical shocks to stimulate the blood flow. I lay there not fully aware of where I was or what I was going on. I felt alone. I needed more answers from the doctor and was waiting for him to come and explain things to me. In the meantime I was content to sleep.

My kids flooded the room to let me know they had been there.

I was grateful to see them but I didn't have happy news.

"The doctor couldn't do the surgery, I said."

I couldn't answer their questions about why not.

Their visit was brief since it was apparent I would be home soon. They were keeping me there overnight as a precautionary measure until the effects of the drugs wore off.

I watched TV and caught a few winks. Other than having an allergic reaction (an itch attack) from the medicine, my night was uneventful. I still couldn't believe I was there in the hospital, had been on the surgical table about to go under the knife, and then everything stopped.

The next morning I was to be discharged after breakfast. I was instructed to shower and get dressed. I still hadn't seen the doctor to receive the full explanation!

I felt abandoned. Left in the lurch. Why hadn't this doctor given me the attention I deserved. He remains a shadow to this day, not fully formed in my mind.

The second doctor that had given me the medical clearance walked in. He was the one with the foreign accent. He was like a breath of fresh air.

"The surgeon couldn't do the operation," he said. "Make sure you talk to him so he can explain what happened."

I said I would. It was what I had been waiting for.

"Maybe it was for the best," he continued. "Maybe something was going to happen and its better that you didn't go through with it."

I was stunned by his words. I had been told by everyone else that this was routine surgery and there was nothing to worry about. I wondered what concerned him.

I returned home and began going about my normal routine, performing my daily tasks walking with a limp and with a hip that was still in pain.

I tried to put the whole situation behind me but something kept nagging at me. One morning it hit me!

I had seen it all before. I had been there before – in that space and time. It had all taken place in my dream!

I reexamined the dream. The doctor was the shadowy figure. I couldn't help but make the connection – the white walls and the lights – the table – the voices in the background.

The second doctor may well have been right. I had thwarted death. But not in the sense I thought I had – but for another reason.

<u>Prayerfully Yours</u>

"I Prayed"

The day of my granddaughter's christening had more than a special meaning. It was a place and time for me to heal. The dream I had was about me! About death. I was forewarned of the events that were to take place.

It was prayer that saved me. That's why I was being drawn towards scripture.

The prayer was totally unexpected. It was the last minute that it was decided to be done. After church and after her christening, grandpa stood up and said:

"Let's pray for your surgery."

We stood. Everyone in the room said a prayer for me. I felt the spirit. When I left I took that special feeling with me.

And even though I had the aura in my bedroom the night before the visit to the hospital – whispering that I might die, that I might not make it – the spirit of the prayer was more powerful, and it was with that feeling that accompanied me as I walked out of the house the next morning. There was no fear, no apprehension. I felt a calmness, even a peace, as I entered the hospital. It had been as if my mind were saying, "If it's meant to be, there's nothing you can do about it."

The dream I feared the most is the one I told my children I would never be able to tell. This one came close.

WHEN CROWS CALL

In The Beginning...

In the beginning I had my dreams. But if the dreams were all I had that would be one thing. But they're not. Along with my dreams there are CROWS. Big crows little crows, crows of all sizes.

My daughter once asked me, "Mother, how do you know it's a crow instead of a raven.

I answered her.

"I just know, alright. Plus, I had done my research."

"What kind of research can you do about crows?" she asked.

"Stuff that just comes to me, that I don't ask for but it comes to me at the right time.

When Crows Call

Upon casual observation of the quirky birds, you wouldn't give much notice. But when they flock around, appear out of nowhere, and constantly intrude on your life, you start to notice a pattern. That's what crows do to me; they follow me around wherever I go, under any circumstances, on any occasion. There is no 'right' time for a crow to show up. There is only a 'necessary' time. I dread when I see them because to me they represent death. They may or may not be friendly, I haven't delved deeply enough to figure that part out. But what I do know now is that, regardless, they are a gift. They are a master of disguise trying to tell a story. They bring me a message and are part of the puzzle I must solve and figure out.

They are an enlightened kind, bringing about encounters that I never ask for. Their message is unfathomable yet clear in its proper context. They are the armor of death and will show up consistently when it occurs.

I can't escape their presence and messages. I have accepted that it is destined for us to be a part of each other forever.

In some ways that seems uncanny, in others it is surreal.

But look at it from my perspective. How do you go around telling people that you have a connection with those birds?

I haven't. And I chose to keep it silent until now. There are many members of my family and many friends who know nothing about this part about me. Why? Because I've chosen to keep it that way. I started out as a young girl having these experiences and only my mother was my confident. Later on it became my kids. And I've found out now, that maybe some of them may have inherited this ability – to be in alignment and read the messages that the crows bring as well as have dreams that are in conjunction with them. Just as one plus two equals three, then Dreams plus Crows equal Death.

The equation is simple in my mind. When the crows show up I have the dreams or vice versa.

The order doesn't matter. It's the pair of them together that does.

The dreams started a long time ago when I was in my teens.

I didn't know how to react to the first dream I had. I ran to my mother for comfort. It went like this…

Dream 1

I was walking along a lonely road on a bright sunny morning. The road was clear except for my two sisters and me. It was a neighborhood street with gray pavement and houses along each side. We were approaching a big blue house in the distance. It had white trim and a tall porch. There were many stairs to climb in order to reach the porch. Details of the inside of the house were sketchy except that it was mostly empty and you could hear your echo through the rooms. A voice was traveling with us. It was a loud voice. I could hear it saying things. Its tone became more forceful and meaner in nature. The voice was saying, "I'll snuff you out!

The sequence of the dream seemed to become scattered.

My sisters had left me and I walked faster to catch up with them. Then, I was alone in the street. There was brightness all around so there wasn't much to be afraid of except the loud voice. I felt isolated and needed to hurry up and look for them. They were already in the house. The big blue house. I walked in the door keeping one foot on the porch. It was as if I were creeping – reluctant to enter. I could see second and third floor in all directions. It was a large wooden house with many rooms. One of my sisters was upstairs. She was the one that the voice was pursuing. The voice had been talking to her the whole trip.

She was still acting in her loud boisterous manner as if the voice didn't phase her. I'm not sure she even heard it. Maybe just I could hear it. Once inside the house my sister had all but disappeared, I could feel her presence but she wasn't there. I was transported from room to room, eventually being taken upstairs. They couldn't hear or see me looking for them.

I heard my sister exiting the house as I hurried to catch up with her. I felt I needed to save her if I could just get there in time. It was too late. I exited the door in a hurry only in time to see my sister heading off in a car. The car was too fast and the person with the loud voice was taking her away.

The voice had been threatening the whole time to silence her but she kept cussing and fussing the entire way. She was 'bad' and no one could harm her. A tough girl, with a tough attitude.

The faces in my dream will not be revealed, nor their names disclosed. But what I can say about it is that what happened next had to do with similar characters.

I went to my mom the next morning having something to get off my chest. I told her that something was going to happen and I felt uneasy about it.

She could see my nervousness as I told her my dream.

My mother had a calm nature and talking to her about anything always put me at ease. She applied the wisdom she was known for and soon soothed me.

"Mama," I said. "What so you think it means? I saw the faces, mama, the people. I saw what happened. I felt it mama."

She looked up at me as we sat at the table.

"Baby, if something is going to happen then there's nothing you can do about it."

I left the table. Out of the corner of my eye I saw a worried look on mama's face.

Later that day, I went with my mom to the discount store. While we were shopping, music was playing the background. I remember that I was standing in the aisle when I heard the news broadcast over the radio.

"A body has been found of a young woman…"

I gasped and ran to my mother.

"Mama, that's my dream, I can feel it!"

We left the store and a few hours later it was confirmed - my cousin – the one known for her 'bad' attitude – had been murdered.

A Link In The Chain

"The Gift"

At some level I always believed I had unique abilities. Things came to me ahead of time. I'm not clairvoyant because if you came to me and asked me what my feelings about some topic represented, specifically, I couldn't tell you.

But premonitions I do have. It is like a pre-thought before the condition occurs.

Dreams are like premonitions. They allow you to see things beforehand. When you are experiencing the dream you are in the moment. You are either on the outside looking in or being a participant.

What's most true about a dream is that you are a different person after having experienced one. You may be able to recall vivid detail or the dream may be scanty or scattered all over the place. The most important thing to remember is that they are a culmination of your experience – present or in the future no matter how disturbing or bizarre they are. That's what I have found out about mine. That the sensory perception I have while sleeping is out of my control. I am unable to channel my dream or hone in on any aspect of it. I can only be in the moment and rely on my recall after the fact.

The link in the chain that I possess is a Gift. I used to question it, wondering if it was a blessing or a curse. But over time I've come to know the true meaning – that 'death' is but a broken link in the chain. And if I have the premonition to see it beforehand, then when it comes to me in a dream, that is a Gift.

History of Crows

During the several years that passed after the first dream, I had many others. Through the course of that time I was fortunate enough to run across a documentary that came on television about crows.

In 2010 I happened upon information describing a documentary that was scheduled to air soon. I marked my calendar. It was to be all about crows.

I was fortunate to catch that episode. I sat attentively hoping for some insight about the birds – something that would speak to why they behaved toward me the way they did. I learned a number of interesting things about them. They are intelligent, ranking next to a primate in comparison to human intelligence. I learned that they were homeopathic in nature. That their familial ties were somewhat like ours. They mate for life and they rear their young over a period of up to five years. I learned that their memory is stellar and they pass on information (warnings) to their young. Their grieving pattern is similar to humans in that they flock at the death site to mourn their own.

This brought me closer to understanding why they may have been there to warn me on so many occasions.

Maybe it was a bird I grew up with. Maybe it was one that followed me from home. Maybe they knew that I had moved away and that our family was close. Maybe they felt a close connection to us. Maybe they were the same birds that traveled from my house to tell me that the end was near for someone. Maybe they knew how I would feel and were grieving, too. They certainly lined up along the telephone wires outside my father's house when he took ill. They told me right then and there that he wasn't going to make it. I love the crows for their care and concern. I no longer fear what was deep inside.

To my amazement I had gotten more than I bargained for. It talked about the crows in details that I could have never imagined.

Dream #2 (my younger cousin)

There was concrete. It curved in a semi-circular fashion as if surrounding a stage. The stairs were graduated but not very deep. It was brightly lit outside on a clear day. I could see my son climbing the steps toward the middle. He appeared to be running from something. At the top he would stop and stand his ground.

Then the scene switched to a busy avenue on the corner. To the side of a familiar looking building a fight was taking place. The person fighting someone was my cousin. His white t-shirt was torn and dirty – perhaps bloody, even. I could not see the other person. My cousin was swinging his fists. He said he wanted to stop fighting but the aggressor kept pursuing him. My cousin won the fight.

Then the scene switched back to the center of the stage where my son was standing. He was agitated and worried, looking over his shoulder as if someone were in pursuit. The scene switched again to my other son wearing a blue plaid shirt, dark sunglasses and laying in a casket. I felt that death had taken place but when I looked closer in the casket the face of my second son turned into the face of my nephew. So, it was my nephew wearing the plaid shirt and dark shades and he was dead.

The dream ended at that point and I woke up in quivers, scared, afraid and distraught over what I had just dreamed. I told my mother about it. Sometime later I remember telling it to my son. He was a teenager at the time and I don't recall his response. A few days later, I learned that my cousin had died. He was killed as he struggled in a fight. I knew upon hearing that, that this was what my dream had been about. When this cousin was killed, several things hit home. His mother had died at the same age he was, and in a similar fashion. She also was in the very first premonition dream I ever had. So in similar ways, it was *deja vu*. I became weary at the thought.

The familial ties, is what I share in common with the birds. I come from a close knit clan too.

The dreams about deaths that I've had have been about family, thus, the broken link. I can feel with a passion when something will happen. In most cases I've seen it before. The crows also come as a pre-sign letting me know that there will be a broken link – that tragedy will follow.

****

Interlude:

A Prayer

Oh how my soul weeps for comfort. Dying inside as I see others suffer. Your Gracious Glory exemplifies me and I am subject to Your Will.

****

I started my day like any other. It was a bit unusual because I had been seeing birds. Not just any birds, the crows. The crows would follow me wherever I went. They'd show up anywhere, anytime, not just for no reason, but for a purpose. The purpose of it all that became clear to me over time. It didn't matter when the crows would come. What mattered was that I couldn't do anything about it. I often reacted with anxiety or by crying or becoming very sad. It was as if lava were about to spew from a volcano, building up until it reached a height of uncontainable proportions.

I experienced a heightened awareness and felt renewed pep in my step. It wasn't because I anticipated something good. Quite the contrary, my nostrils would flare and my head would rear like a horse on a mission. My throat would swell and my eyes were ready to well because I knew at any moment something terrible could happen.

That was the teaser that the birds gave me. If, as has so often been said, ravens are mad, then crows must be crazy. That's the way I looked at it. They are crazy for going out of their way to bring me a message.

I wondered so many things. Who was I? Why was I so special? What made me worthy of this interchange? These were the questions I had about the birds. And more importantly the questions I had for God. God had sent the birds. Who else could have? I had been asking myself thaht over and over again for such a long time. If they were a medium (of exchange) then what was my role (as a recipient)? Those thoughts plagued me for years, eating away at the very fabric of my being.

I questioned the process, and I questioned why they showed up. I knew that when they came, their message was clear; there was no denying that. The message was that someone would soon fall victim to harm or foul play. Someone was going to die or even be murdered, and that's a fact!

It was hard to fathom – this living with these birds all my life – but I walked with them in dignity and admiration. How could I not grasp the magnitude of what they meant to me let alone the messages that they were bringing. It continues to be awesome! It is a gift!

A gift of sort, – even if unwanted – but a gift nonetheless.

I wonder if my mother understood that I had a gift when I used to tell her my stories. My Dreams come from Deep Places – REM sleep, I believe they call it. The dark recesses of your mind that's unknown to you when you sleep. That's what the crows meant to me – they knew my tale.

What was it that made me quiver at the thought of telling someone else about my experiences – my relationship with the crows and with my dream world? My body would retreat, withdrawing as if to preserve its innocence. That's what I was you know, an innocent victim. A pawn in a deadly game – process – over which I had no control.

My Dreams seemed useless if I couldn't act on them to save somebody. Wondering who it could be or imagining what could come next – those were the most spine tingling thoughts one could have. How dare I think that the worst was going to happen. What happened to putting the best spin on life's events? That has always been my basic, happy nature…and…why? Why was I chosen as an instrument of dissemination (instead of someone else). My body was fragile and carrying the burden often seemed too heavy to bear. I longed for my load to be lightened. But how could I be lifted out of this dark chamber of repetitive morbidity?

My mind searched frantically for ways of escaping. But the more I tried, the more things came back. They were often cloaked as beasts shrouded in the night.

I had been seeing crows for a week before the Dream.

I made a comment to my children: "The crows are showing up, you know what that means."

Everyone was on heightened alert. Is mom getting ready to drop a bombshell? And, yes, I was….

Two crows stood out in particular. One the night before I had the dream, and the other one that changed its configuration.

This bird had been outside my door all day. If I peeked out the window or walked to my car, it made a point to land in front of me every time. I couldn't dodge the bird so there was no point in trying. This one was clearly seeking intimate quarters with me. My uneasiness about the birds had me sleeping light as a feather. My heart kept pounding, waiting for something to happen.

At night, I lay fearful, waking frequently. The fan was blowing on me. I needed the coolness of it to ward off the summer heat. I didn't understand where the fear was coming from. I was, by nature, not a tense person. I would shut my eyes tightly only to have them snap wide open again. Once, when opened, I was staring at the figure of a bird. The fan was black, the bird was black – was that a coincidence? The bird had shown up in my bedroom transposing itself with the fan. My window was open but it had a screen. I was high on the second floor but there was no room for any animal to perch. The sliding aluminum framed windows wouldn't accommodate that. My blink became a stare as I my eyes widened and I looked longer and harder at the bird. It flicked its wings as if to disappear and that's when I saw it. The Grimm reaper! I was frozen. My body wouldn't move. That was the moment I remembered the story my mother told me when I was little.

I never asked her what that meant but saw it in full swing when my three year old nephew was screaming frantically at things only he could see.

"The spiders, he yelled, they're gonna get me?"

He was yelling and screaming and stomping around, clearly terrified. My mother grabbed him and held him tightly to her bosom.

It was as if he were in a trance. My mother pretended to be stomping and made gestures as if beating the spiders and shooing them away. She rocked him gently and a state of calm soon allowed him peace again.

That's how I felt. As if something had a hold over me. I was frightened. The black hood over the skeletons face stood out. The scythe was in its hand below the hood. It acted like it was coming to claim someone, but who? My body wanted to move, but couldn't. I was screaming for help inside my head, but the sound wouldn't manifest itself through my lips. My children were fast asleep in the other room.

After quite some time, I managed to pull myself together. My body slowly edged from the position in which I had been laying. The frightening feeling stayed with me, however. The scythe disappeared almost as suddenly as it had appeared and the hooded figure turned back into a fan. I couldn't sleep the rest of the night. That experience confirmed to me that death was stalking.

The dream I will describe had come one night before the grim reaper dream.

The Dream #3

A fish was swimming in a tub. It was a small fish at first but kept getting bigger and bigger. Dana, my grandbaby, was in the tub playing with the fish. It kept growing until Dana was no longer playing with it. Her laughter turned into fear. Growing larger and larger it began jumping back and forth between two tubs. Another bathtub had emerged in the bathroom and they were side by side, just a few feet separating them. Dana was slipping further and further away but I couldn't see where she was going. It seemed that she was shrinking more and more and disappearing in the water. The splashing continued and became more forceful. It was as if the fish was enjoying thrusting its body back and forth between the tubs. My heart wept as Dana sank.

The words that rang in my mind were: "Someone needs to get the baby!" I kept saying it over and over. I asked someone if they had gotten the baby but they did not reply. No one other than the fish and the baby had been present in the dream, not even me. It had just been the fish and the baby – the baby that eventually drowned. I remember the sad feeling that overwhelmed me at the end of the dream. At that point I wanted to retract everything I had seen. But I couldn't. There was no amount of rewinding that would work. As I began to rouse from the dream, I whispered to myself that it wasn't true. But, in truth, the unshakable feeling of something awful was upon me once again.

Since my nephew's death I had had three dreams. A pattern was developing. I was not ready to accept my calling. I needed more time – more time to assimilate what was really happening. I was convinced at that point, that I was a Link in a Chain. It was a long chain of ancestors that were connected. It couldn't have started with me. I questioned it. There had to be others. Or did there? I felt like blood was being spilled on my watch. I bore the responsibility, and somehow stood the blame.

Mama knew about every one of the dreams. I had told her every detail of my dreams-before-the event occurred.

There was a saying that she used to say and it was later adopted by son and the other children:"Oh, no! . . . Not another!" My mother and sons reaction had evolved over time as well. At first they had responded with attentiveness and intrigue by sitting on the edge of their seat or forcing the phone close to their ear as I told them. But when reality set in, that these Dreams were actually coming true, they sat more reluctantly as if wanting to cover their ears. I could sense their reluctance and fears.

What use is a medium if you can't make predictions? Dreams are like having precognitive abilities but not being able to act on them. And crows are like signs in the road that you don't know how to follow. Which one means go? Which one means stop? Which one is marked for death?

When blood is spilled, I can't explain or understand how I knew in advance. That's why I never shared my gift with others outside of my family. I would be a freak, I thought. But I have come to peace with it. And that's why the pen has met the paper here for all to see. It is time to share my life, my story and my encounters with the unknown. Maybe there are others like me, and hearing my story those others might be moved to tell theirs.

You have to think about it first – or maybe you don't. Maybe you just know (it's intuitive). "What medium has consistently shown up for me – to warn me about things?" It would be in my personal space and possibly no one else can see. That medium may be uncomfortable at times or give you disturbing thoughts. But it is there to agitate you and point you in a direction. It is for you to determine what direction that is.

I always said the Greatest fear I had is the dream I would never be able to tell.

At the beginning of this book, I relayed to you the Dream, 'Eyes Wide Open'. That is the dream that came closest for me!

I didn't spend much of my time worrying about what people might say. I just didn't tell them. I didn't talk about it or even bring it up because it's not exactly the conversation you can have, say, over a cup of tea – it sounds a bit morbid, talking about death and its precursors.

For a long time I wondered, why me? Why was I chosen to be the vehicle by which this information came? And the crows; what exactly did they have to do with it?

I had more of my answers after I took a trip to the park one day.

CHAPTER TWO

THEY COME BACK

It was a short while after my nephew had passed. My family was still grieving. Taking the kids to the park was a good distraction. Besides, they needed more breathing room and time out of the confines of my small apartment.

Southern California is spacious and beautiful. There were plenty of places we could have gone to or chosen that day for recreation. I looked for a park nearby because although I had wanted to go, I was low on energy and really didn't feel up to it. But keeping two small children happy outweighed everything else.

As I drove, I passed several of parks. Nothing seemed 'funsway', as they call it. Normally, I would have stopped at the first one trying to get it over with, but something kept urging me to drive on. Just at the point of giving up and turning around, I found that I had driven down a wrong street. It was one I wasn't familiar with. I had to make a u-turn in order to turn around and get back to the main avenue, I was able to do that at the end of the block. There, sitting off to my right, neatly tucked away, was a beautiful little park. It was quiet and inviting. I pulled over and parked. Who would have ever known that such a quaint little park would have been hidden here at the end of a *cul-de-sac*, and so close to home.

The narrow pathway, which led into the park was wedged between two buildings. We could see the playground off in the distance and that's where my daughter and her two kids headed. I decided to stay in the car and relax along with my younger daughter who was in the backseat reading. It was a nice quiet afternoon with the sun beaming down on us. I propped my feet up to take a nap. I had no intention of moving or getting out. I was set to catch some zzz's while they were playing.

Sleep didn't come. After a while boredom set in. I needed to stretch my legs. I got out of the car and began to walk. My daughter followed dragging her feet a bit. A building on the right caught my eye. I discovered an open door and automatically entered it as if I knew what I was doing. I had no idea what lay behind that door until I stepped inside. There was a pool table, and maybe foosball or some similar game. A TV was perched high in one corner and someone was sitting with their back to us watching it.

I glanced at the other two people in the room. They appeared to be working there. My daughter and I played a game of pool. Nothing serious, just messing around. I don't think we were even keeping score. In the middle of the game we were approached by a young man. I heard his voice before I saw his face. The man came over smiling and stroking his goatee. He laughed and joked making light conversation. I don't even remember his exact words, but it was his voice that stood out. He sounded just like my nephew. That's what prompted me to look up.

"You sound just like my cousin," my daughter said to him.

Then he began making gestures in a fashion similar to my nephew. He stroked his beard, cracked jokes and laughed. My mouth dropped open. Then he started being playful with my teenage daughter. Their interaction reminded me of her with her older cousin. I couldn't believe my eyes nor what was happening. I looked at the young man closer and told him that he was the spitting image of my nephew, except a younger version. He kept a smile on his face the whole time. Then he walked over toward the young lady that had her back turned to us watching TV. They started talking.

My daughter and I left the game room amazed. When we reached the playground, I told my older daughter about the encounter and asked her to return with us so she could see him. She gathered her children and we headed back. At that moment we saw the young man crossing the path ahead of us moving from one building into the other.

"There he is, see!" I said excitedly.

But she didn't get a good look at him, nor was she privy to the interaction we had. He had disappeared behind a closed door. We kept a watchful eye out hoping he would return. As we were making ready to leave the park, I tried the handle on the door he had entered. It was locked. I was puzzled about how he exited.

After that incident, I felt compelled to tell my sister. But I couldn't find it within me to bring up the part about seeing her son since she had just recently lost him. Instead, I drafted an email when I got home and sent it to my niece. I needed to tell them that he was okay. I told them the whole situation and how it transpired. How we were reluctant to go to the park. How no one wanted to get out. How there was no one else in the park nor the recreation room except the young lady that worked there and the young man that appeared out of nowhere but also apparently worked there.

After that encounter, I was convinced of the connection I had with my family. I understood my purpose and that I was to act as a medium. This was the second time one of my loved ones had come back to make contact with me to let me know they were okay. It had been a powerful showing of him in the flesh.

Sometime later we went back to the park again hoping to see him. He never showed up again. The doors on the building were locked and there was no one we could ask.

The purpose of that whole trip on that particular day had been to bring me closer to my nephew so that I could pass the message on that he was okay.

Two things happened differently that time from before:

1. My younger daughter was present and witnessed what I saw.

2. That I told someone other than my children about it.

When my Daddy came back, I didn't know right away that's what was happening. He pulled me directly to him and I felt his spirit spreading through me.

The last place I saw my Daddy was where he and I dropped a tear. I held my Daddy's hand almost to the end as others in my family were also fortunate to do. He squeezed my hand as he lay there in his hospital bed. I felt the love he has given me as one of his children. I walk with that love in my heart everyday.

On the day that I was coming back to attend his funeral, something strange happened. I was driving my car on a freeway that was quite familiar to me from my childhood. A freeway exchange appeared ahead. For some reason I took it. It had not been my plan. That wasn't the direction I was headed. I was trying to get to my parents house. It would seem empty with the passing of my father. Nothing in the city would be the same for me.

I passed several exits before taking one with the intention of turning around. The exit I had taken felt just as strange as the section of freeway I was traveling at the time. Then, a series of odd things took place. I felt like I was no longer navigating the steering wheel. To turn around should have been easy but it wasn't. All I needed to do was head over the ramp and reverse direction. But my mind wasn't being steered to do that. It was as if my mind was oblivious to what I was doing.

Sometime later I found myself in front of the hospital. I could feel my Daddy's spirit moving me – calling me. I could feel that my

Daddy was still there and that his spirit had never left. It was the last place that I had seen him alive. And there I was in front of the emergency exit of the hospital. That was my turn around point. I paused for a few minutes as I realized I had been taken there. I shed a tear and spoke a few words to my Daddy.

"I miss you Daddy. I understand now. I know it was you that brought me here. I love you".

I will always remember that hospital the way it appeared when I last saw my father and how he summoned me there.

When I finally did make it to my parent's home I related the entire experience to my mother. I said that I had made a detour I hadn't expected. I told her that Daddy was okay and had drawn me toward him. My mother with her calm demeanor responded as she always did – as if she understood. Her eyes brightened through her grief.

As I slept in their house for those few days, I felt that Daddy wasn't there, that he was still at the hospital. Maybe his soul hadn't reached there yet, or maybe he had told me to send a message to my mother.

Follow up visits such as that one with my Daddy aren't strange to me. But when my mother died, I looked for one. When my two nephews died they came back. But what about my mother? I was very close to her. We had a ritual that we shared with the dreams. For her not to arrive (come back) makes me wonder if I'm being deprived of a happy medium. After all, she was my closest ally. My mother understood all the pain and beguiling I had behind this. So why haven't I gotten a visit? Why hasn't my mother come back to see me or tell me that she is okay?

Or maybe the question should be, who am, that I should ask? My mother was a peaceful woman. She died with her children by her side like my Daddy. She departed this world knowing that all her children were alive and well. What more could a mother ask for? I certainly don't question it. Why haven't we had such an interchange. Because I carry her in my heart with each footstep I take. Mourn no more for me she is saying, because I will always be with You.

In a way I felt that my cousin had come back. She didn't manifest the same way as the others, but through her son. When he was killed it showed her presence. Gone but not forgotten. I felt that she came to claim her son. Maybe she was gone too soon, maybe she didn't have enough time with him, but I found it ironic that he died at the same age as she did and in almost the same manner.

God Giveth and God taketh. And when God claimed their souls, they were connected together once again.

***

Gone doesn't mean gone forever. Gone means present in a

different place and time. All is not lost if you no longer have contact with your loved one. Sometimes they are able to communicate on a higher frequency.

When my nephew came back, I could see him clearly. He was high above me not touching the ground. As I looked at him I could see the colors of the clothes he was wearing. He was there for only a few moments.

"Tell my mother I'm okay," he said.

I didn't hesitate to run and give her the message. I felt the joy of his presence.

The clearness that's present, we call it air or space. I call it a veil that meshes together two completely separate worlds. The clarity we should have for understanding that this other world exists should be the same as the clearness we witness everyday right before our eyes. I can't help but think our presence is felt to them as well. Otherwise, how could they see us and know to communicate.

They come to you as they were before because that's how you knew and accepted them. But it's pretty obvious that there's a greater force at play.

I accepted the challenge of understanding what my nephew's presence meant and knew that that there was a greater importance to his message. He was giving a healing message. One that would comfort his mother's soul while he was no longer in her presence.

The Crows, The dreams, My loved ones returning to me...there was a clear pattern. I was a heartbeat, like a drum, in the clan. Any tug at that force, or that link, I could feel. Any break in the chain, was for me to know. Knowledge about any passage or return was for me to disseminate.

    Putting it all together clarified my role and added substance to my life.

CHAPTER THREE

EXPLORING DREAMS

Dream (class)

Fairy tales can present a happy ending because you have control over the outcome. So do fantasies. They can seem real because that is the way you want them to be. But dreams are different. A Dream is an altered state of consciousness.

You have heard the phrase, "Don't bust my bubble." That one sentence suggests that you want to remain in the state you are experiencing as a sense of euphoria. In your world, everything is perfect as you have imagined it. Perfect for you. If you share that thought or fantasy that you're having, someone else may not share the same sentiment. One comment or action can shatter that realm that you hold so precious and dear.

Dreams are different. They can't be altered, retold or rewritten, except as we imagine them. Dreams are reels that are playing in your head providing live action while you sleep. You are there in the moment, experiencing it that way.

My dreams are powerful and began when I was a young girl. The dreams that stood out and were the most memorable were the dreams of death and people reaching out for help. I can remember them vividly and they provide a connection to my living world.

The studies that have been done about dreams are interesting. They can now be classified and given whole new meanings in many categories thus stirring controversy as common threads are identified. Dream interpretation has become an entity in and of itself, providing a road map and linkage to another world.

Nightdreaming and Daydreaming are both done in our restful state. We are sleeping and yet we remain conscious. Our brain activity is in overdrive and gearing up towards confrontation. We must confront ourselves upon awakening and at least try to discover who we are, or at least as our last dream had defined us. Grasping your thoughts and trying to remember every detail can be hard unless your dream is so powerful it compels you to do so.

That's why interpreting them is important and why for centuries people have been trying to figure them out.

I went to a dream class once because I wanted to understand them better. I didn't actually seek out a dream interpretation class. But just like coming upon the documentary about the crows was happenstance, so was my encounter with the person telling me about the dream class. That person had no clue that I was having troubles figuring out mine. The earth has a way of aligning itself with your needs. And sometimes you end up thrust into its bowels. I welcomed the opportunity to attend the class.

I got more than I bargained for. I had never before delved into what anyone's dreams meant, let alone that there were multiple sources of interpretation. This information came in the nick of time for me. It was one more body of information that could help me move closer to understanding what I was experiencing. I attended the class with high hopes. Although the women in attendance were quite pleasant and obviously had been doing this for a long time, I didn't feel the need to go back. I didn't share their sentiments I suppose. I wasn't looking for a lost love or exploring relationships. They were looking for someone to interpret their future while I was looking for someone to explain my past. Needless to say, there was no Mahatma Gandhi in the room. There had been no enlightening moment and I left there feeling as frustrated as when I came. What I did take away from there was that there are a whole host of possibilities for interpretations of dreams. So why not stick with what I already know - that dreams are real, and that they do come true.

***

Emotionally, I was fragile as a piece of paper, yet pliable as rubber. The resilience I have developed from experiencing my dreams has been my mainstay. I have walked with a secret for years and only those that were privileged in my family knew about it. My confidants had to be trusted souls and not people who would speak about it randomly or take it lightly.

They were sharing my burden and were brought into my realm of influence. The intonations, the fluctuation in their voice, their racing heart beat and facial expressions all told me how they were reacting at the time. If I sensed a hint of hesitation in someone, then he could not be privy to my story. If I felt someone could brush it off as lightweight as if not meaning anything, then I would stop. Those sorts would be denied the privilege of knowing the sacredness of what I was trying to convey.

When my mother or son showed hesitation over time, it wasn't as a reluctance on their part to hear my dreams, it was a pause, ever so briefly, to gear up for what was coming. They did not take the message lightly. They understood the magnitude of the situation. Opening oneself up to want to know about something Bad or Good that's going to happen could make you vulnerable. And it also makes you share the burden of the messenger.

I never did this on purpose, having to tell someone. It was always like an earthquake building up inside and I felt compelled to let go, to let it break through. It wasn't I that was moving the earth. I was the vehicle. I released the information that Dreams and the Crows conveyed. My heart felt less pressure afterward, less strain. The agitation was still there, even the anxiety. But I was relieved, nonetheless.

I would imagine that the burden I was having them shoulder could make them feel the same way. That's why I never underestimated how precious they were in listening to me, in being my participants. We all walked in silence. And after the initial message was told, it was never brought up again. There could be no, "I told you so," after the events played out. The feeling was more like,

"I wish this had never happened. I wish my dreams hadn't been real."

After the shock of finding out who the real victim was, there was no longer any point to piecing it together. The stage had been set. The dream had been experienced, and the steps leading up to it were all going to play out. There was no way of stopping the force or magnitude of it. I knew that. My burden bearers knew it. And we had discovered it with time. The bouts of relief between dreams could be years, even decades.

Clearness/Veil/Thief in the Night

Beyond Our Capacity

Things that are clear (they call it see through) are:

The <u>Air</u> is clear

The <u>Atmosphere</u> (space) is clear

<u>Water</u> is clear and <u>Glass</u>

Our breath is clear as it exits our body and travels through space and time. It sends ripples and currents like bodies of water or softly blown wind.

If it were not for the medium we have chosen to harness it and reflect it, it would remain traveling until it dissipates. Everything is coming from the mind which is at the center of it. Our brain is the control mechanism. Once our brain stops functioning we no longer exist in this body. The Big Question is, do we maintain and continue in some form of existence beyond the worldly form. I have seen the other side and have glimpsed that it exists.

---Familiar---

What was familiar to me were voices. The chatter of those I knew huddled in a space. It was a space that we occupy with them simultaneously. They can see us clear as day however, we can only see them when that contact is made or that veil is lifted by them. Two worlds meshed together like our voices traveling in wind. We can't see, touch or feel it unless *it* manifests.

That sixth sense tells us when something is there. You can feel the presence and sometimes even see it. It is captured like in a bottle momentarily enough for you to recognize it. You cannot communicate with it or explain this phenomenon. You simply know that its there like the images that show up on your television screen. You have caught the shadow and images of others. Their voice is a reflection of having traveled through space and time.

We meet others that we may have otherwise never known were it not radio or TV. So traveling thru time and space is not a foreign phenomena. Nor are the thoughts that visit our minds awakening us and arousing our senses. We react similarly because we are of One Kind. The thought that is carried through, passes to another and so on with all of our actions. As a species of One Kind it is our reactions that tell us who we are. We reflect the voices and winds of currents – that which is traveling through us. It is of no surprise that the entities exist. They are taking up another shape and form. One that is not foreign or alien to us, but one that is beyond what we can see unless that opportunity is given to us.

When I saw and heard the people that surrounded me I wasn't frightened. I was, however, laying there like a specimen unable to participate unless I got up and followed the light. It was as if I had to move toward the light to go beyond and see more. But the voices were letting me know that I wouldn't come back. "Should we take her," one said. The voices were all talking at once - similar to people gathered in a room, huddled together talking with their voices indistinguishable except for the one that said what I heard. I could feel the movement of their bodies so knew they were present. What I don't know was if the hand that was reaching down was being directed by what that voice was saying or acting alone – sneaking, while the others weren't paying attention. I couldn't tell if it was a warning to me as if saying, 'Look what I can do. The answers you seek I can show you, but it would come with the price of your life. The form in which you are currently living will be over. You would have to join us in this place, this other world, this other existence in order to understand what you seek to know.'

I woke up at the very moment the clearness (or cellophane) was being pressed over my mouth and being sucked in by my breath. Then it dissipated as the figure was pulling back. I heard a swooping noise- a swishing sound. The glimpse of what I saw had occurred with my eyes wide open and my mind in disbelief. That was the moment I knew it was real.

So as we continue to walk, talk or move – surrounded by the clearness – we must also be aware that there are those that occupy the clearness among us. And that they can see us as plainly as we've come to know they exist. It is like the bridge divide where the two worlds open showing up at the right time when you have questions and when you are deep in thought about life, the world and all that is in it. When your thoughts travel far enough in space and time to transfer the brightness towards you that is held as a pathway to that which we think is Beyond our capacity of comprehension.

To touch feel and exist in that other world we must be in it. The shield (veil) that holds us apart is not of our choosing. And it is only the Entity that made us that can show us through that Barrier. Even beyond, however, in my dream, I noticed that we must still seek permission. For the question -"Should I take her?' - let me know that. But what I was given proof of is that all is not lost. And that gone doesn't mean gone forever.

It means Bridging to and existing in another world – possibly in another shape or form (although I didn't get that impression) and being able to communicate with those that are familiar.

With that experience, I have become at peace about knowing where I am headed and that I must taste death to get there. And that death can be quiet and still and taken while I'm sleeping.

I can understand why people have Blind Faith. They are tuning in with that sixth sense and acknowledging that something larger than Life – more than what they know – Exists. There are signs all around us. These are communications that enter our thoughts and minds through different channels and mediums. Most are in the form of something tangible – another person, a TV, a computer or a radio. But how does it get there? That is the unseen that is Beyond Us. It travels through time and space as we do as a form of communication. Something that ties us together forever as one of a kind. It is a reaching out to others to try to understand the similarities in their Groupings as well (other animals, or live beings).

Prayer and meditation, channeled in such a way as to wonder about the vastness of it all – seeking Answers – is to be shown what it all is about! Why do we exist and will we continue to exist after this body dwindles away? We are constantly seeking the Answers to these and much more. And as our discovery has shown us, it gets easier over time as we continue to scout our way.

Yet it all can be wiped out in an instant no matter what progress or how far we think we have come. So, should that be fear of the unknown or contemplation of the inevitable – that we will continue to exist – but not in the way as we know it.

Contrived faith will continue to be block our understanding. Our existence is Beyond our Capacity of Comprehension, We must acknowledge that.

To fully comprehend means to taste death, even if it is only the initial part of our transformation. The Brightness must be there to demonstrate that Clearness is absence of Forethought. A Clear Blank White Wall shows nothing on it and that Nothing should be put up as a prop to bridge our way. Only God has the capacity to show us Clearly where we're headed and what This all is For!

Opposites exist. In between the opposites is the Clearness. When these two collide an interruption is present. A divide exists. Something is holding up the separation until it is time to let the guard down and those two will cancel each other out. Will that be the End, when opposites collide? I have no knowledge that that is a bridge to our further existence. I have no proof that I must see that form of destruction to enter into the Brightness. That's why it is foolish for anyone to believe it has the capacity to conquer the other. Can't they see that ultimately both sides, when they have once crossed that divide, will cancel each other out? And a new life will spring forth. It is what Spring is all about because out of death comes life and through life comes death. It is an equation that leads to the Ultimate Answer - Do we live on? Yes we live on and can possibly live forever. We spring back and morph ourselves in many forms. Taking on the shapes and forms of the entities with which we share our DNA. Everlasting life will continue until the Clearness is Shone, the Bright path is taken, and that last breath is stolen as a thief in the night. That's when you know your existence will be transformed from one form into another. But first you must follow the light to join the voices that you may hear in the room.

CHAPTER FIVE

LETTER TO OPRAH

What's Oprah Got To Do With It?

One morning I was getting excited about a powerful message I had been receiving and long since wanting to share.

I was thinking about how to reach the largest audience and possibly connect with others like me. I thought about Oprah because of the types of broadcasts she does and that she is capable of reaching a wide audience.

I said to myself:"I will ask her to help me publish my book and get this information to the world."

I sat down and drafted a letter.

Oprah, I started. "I am writing you because . . ."

[*I need your help. I have a story I want to tell and it must reach everybody. It is about personal experience, death, and all the intrigue that surrounds a good tale. I'm not trying to pull the sista card, but a sister needs a break! My story is true. I have written it in the form of a memoir. I cry every time I reminisce, it and know you will too.*

Oprah, there are others like me and I want to find them.

Clairvoyant, visionaries, however we want to label it. But the crows have played a big part in my life as well as the dreams ever since I was a little girl. I am now 52 years old and my kids have encouraged me to write about it. I have sent you a copy of my manuscript in hopes that you will find it worthy of publishing. I know if it gets the Oprah stamp of approval it will have a wide affect. Plus it will be interesting to see who emerges forward having only held back for fear of being labeled different. I don't mind the label. I embrace my calling. And although I haven't figured out what it means with your help I can maybe find the answer.

Oprah, I love you as a person and I love your show. I love how you bring out the best in people no matter at what cost i.e.(the risk of embarrassment, shame or being shunned, etc.). I value your courageousness in the face of adversity and that is why I make my appeal. Plus, quite frankly Oprah-A sista needs a break!

My plea: a. Please, help me publish my book

b. Please help me find others who may be like me.

Oprah I believe it is a story worth sharing with the world!]

After the letter was drafted I tucked it away excitedly anticipating the moment when I could send it. I didn't want to be premature because my book wasn't completed yet. I felt at that time that it only needed a few polishing touches to get it into proper book form. But to my surprise a lot had taken place since then. New chapters were to be written, new knowledge, insight and experience were to be gained. The Book was taking on a life of its own because I am living it as we speak. I wondered if at some point there could be an END. I surmised that I would finalize where I am so far in that process. The book must culminate but not on my time, on Gods time.

More and more events took place and came to fill these pages. Many years would pass before I realized that my dream had come true - my dream of being on Oprah and meeting others like me. It was only after watching her series Lifeclass and Super Soul Sunday did I realize that this had happened. I watched all of her life classes religiously because they were awe inspiring and I was drawn to them.

I had missed half of the first show of Super Soul Sunday. I saw a man riding in a car talking about how he felt about God and then his fiance talked about him. It was enough to make me watch every other episode, waking up early on Sundays to do so. I would sit for the three hours learning something new each time or at least reaffirming something I'd already run across. Either way, they were very good shows.

About a week after her last show had aired, my daughter called me to inform me that a rerun of the Super Soul Sunday series was beginning the following week. She reminded me that it was the first episode that both she and I had missed and she wanted to see it from the beginning. I told her I really hadn't thought anymore about it because what I had seen of that episode I thought was sufficient - and maybe even was the best part.

She said, "I'm coming over early to watch it, are you gonna be up?"

I was up. I opened the door for her at five a.m.

We sat to watch together. As the show proceeded, I was drawn into it. The more the man was about revealing his experiences - the more I related to it. But it wasn't until the end of the show that I realized a profound moment – my prayers had been answered.

I realized that piece of paper that I had tucked away almost a year before (the letter to Oprah) represented my dream. I had written it hurriedly with passion and conviction and at the same time tucking it away as if it were a treasure.

I laughed with my daughter when I told her about that lifeclass episode where the lady had buried her letter in the dirt hidden away until she came to retrieve it years later. I also mentioned how it's ironic that I had watched every episode of Super Soul Sunday except that very first part. I told her how the best had been saved for last and there was a reason for it. I said, I wasn't supposed to see that part until my book was completed. I told her that my book was already written. I laughed, explaining to her that I would now need to write another letter to Oprah thanking her for what she had done. And although it wasn't I that was on her show, my prayers had been answered and my dream had come true. Through her show, I met others like me, which is what I had hoped and prayed for the most. And it was through watching that last (or the first) episode that I had realized it!

So everything does serve a purpose in our seeking of light – the Crows, the Dreams, the signals we get from others as they are used as mediums (vessels) when they cross our paths.

I have learned my lesson well and although I am on a continuum, I have come to realize that Life Begets Life and Everything of Life Comes out of death.

And I believe that we do continue on and that our light never goes out but will continue to burn long after we come to exist in another form.

So the dream that I will never tell, I no longer fear.

Because of the light and all that I have come to know, I will approach it as a blank slate, (as God had revealed to me in my dream) with nothing preconceived or contrived and let the Light and the voices lead the way!

You don't think after a while - it is what it is

It's not like you go around acting differently or telling everybody about your experiences. You go about your days as usual. There is no paranoia except around the time right after I have a dream. That may be because the event in our physical world hasn't happened yet.

I later grew into the understanding that I would rather have connection with those that praise God than those who didn't, because I felt more comfortable with that energy (high). At least their focus is trying to connect with God.

Another aspect of talking about it (the dreams)

It can be over-talked because it can be overwhelming to the person that's hearing it to the point of being labeled a borderline kook (crazy). When someone tries to make it feel that way, that's when you need to shut it down - that's when you let it be, let it rest and realize it is what it is.

A Means To An End

Am I special?

Finding myself in all of this was confusing because I didn't know if it was a blessing or a curse. I used to question it, what I now call, "The Gift", because all I used to see was the bad part of it.

If I have the abilities to see things ahead of time in my dreams then why can't it be for something good - like winning the lottery or something. Surely something great was going to happen that would be joyful and worth celebrating (knowing about it in advance). I already had made the connection, that it was to my family, so why not know about it?

There were many memorable happy occasions that occurred in my family. I just wasn't privy to know about them ahead of time or have had a dream about them.

We usually plan our joyful moments like, birth, marriage, career promotion, raises, etc. and make them part of our celebration. But death, like the outcome of birth is unpredictable.

Not until they are born do we know who our children are going to be or what they'll look like. Similarly, death-to many of us, happens unrepentantly. Not knowing when or how we're going to die is beyond us.

Death is usually upon us before we notice it and by then, it is often too late.

That's why not being able to intervene after knowing something is about to happen can be perplexing. It's a nail biting and hair raising experience.

Although I didn't live my life as such, when the events occurred, that's how I reacted.

What I realize is that there's no need for disrespecting the different labels we have. They are all a form of connecting. It is up to each of us to find that which we are being drawn toward. No one can define that but you, regardless of what outside sources you seek to help define it. Connecting with Christianity and being drawn toward the Bible, Islam, Buddhism - aren't as relevant as the connection itself. Your facts - heart felt or not - define your exposure, not the cumulative of who you are or the connection. That is the very reason I am less drawn towards rituals than I am to channeling the energy – that energy that demonstrates that God Exists and that it is Beautiful.

So make your connection. Draw on that with which you're familiar or which gives you the greatest understanding. But don't define it as the End or tell all of your situation. In other words, don't let rituals define you.

My spiritual Energy was increased a notch because of my experiences. I believe all people have them - the experiences. But when I find out who I am, like most people, I'll tell you. I live my life on a continuum. There is no end in sight, just many more questions.

Religion represents to me a Means to An End, while I'm looking for an End to a Means. That's why I always outgrow anything I have been exposed to regarding rituals and what not. Not that it doesn't get deep, because it does, but because I don't want to be confined in a box saying that that's all there is or that's all God is when I know God is much bigger than that (bigger than any religion.).

My daughter once asked me< " At what age did you start your spiritual quest? Before which kid?"

I said, "When I was young. It started before I had kids. I was always searching."

My life had been so messed up before that, there was nowhere to go but up – chalk that up to just being a kid, or growing pains. I was a confused child with a sense of moral consciousness. I felt I had to have all my children even though they weren't under the most ideal circumstances. I was wild and free, untamed, like a love child. I was looking for love in all the wrong places.

Regardless of the rituals we choose, it results in an offering of the spirit or mind. It is also about asking for forgiveness, or it is about wanting something you feel is missing. So the ritual itself is a means to an end. It is also an appeasing of the soul.

My daughter asked me: "What is your best space - the beach huh?"

She proposed her own answer.

I replied: "Yes-I could be there all day and do nothing else. I could be a beach bum and do nothing else in life. That's how soothing the ocean is to me."

She laughed but understood the truth in it.

Signs

- It wasn't an accident, its not a coincidence:

-When the bird pecked the lady

-When the crows lined up on the telephone wire above my parents house to warn me that my Daddy wouldn't make it

-When I saw the silhouette of my son in law on the stairs (but he really wasn't there) and then appeared there much later

-When the very large crow showed up in Germany in order to stand out against the white snow and be seen

-When I had an unsettling dream that made me nervous and worried in Germany

-When my grand daughter had the dream and not I

-When I was in the store shopping and knew from the radio it was someone close to me that was killed without even hearing the name

-When I was drawn back to the hospital where my Daddy was

-When my nephew came to tell me he was okay

-When my next nephew came to do the same

_When we were drawn to a particular park for no apparent reason

_When I had the dreams the night before and then saw the figure

_When I was questioning God and all there is about life and was drawn to scripture

-When my surgery seemed like it never happened and then it didn't

-When my Daddy called me to his room (hospital)

-When the surgery was redone, it was not without consequence as pre-told in my dream

----

The Second Surgery

Just when I had given up hope that anything was going to happen regarding the hip and arthritis, I received a letter in the mail asking me to give an orthopedic doctor a call. My reluctance was well founded considering what I had gone through. I waited about a week before I called the office and spoke with a nurse. I asked who the doctor was and why I should see him?

"You have every right to be apprehensive considering what happened. I'm not sure why the other doctor couldn't do your surgery, but its up to you whether or not you want to see this doctor to see If he can perform it."

Things relating to the procedure were starting to come into focus and names and faces began to get real. This was in stark contrast to the preparations for the first attempt. I met with the doctor.

He really felt confident that he could do the surgery. I had no reason to believe that he could, but at the same time figured that had nothing to lose. I was already living with the aches and pains of my ailments. In the worse case scenario, I would remain the same – in pain and with limited mobility. However, the last thing I wanted was to be put on that table again, knocked out, and then told that I couldn't have the surgery. There was no amount of reassuring this doctor could give me to make me go forward with it. If it were to happen it would be because I still had faith that it could be successful, given the right set of circumstances and the right team of experts. And even though I was high risk, I was still willing to put myself to the test.

I had given it a lot of thought and told my children that if I didn't make it there were things I wanted them to do. Namely, be good, respect one another and always keep the family together; that was important to me.

This doctor was a naturalist and although gray headed he was much younger then the first doctor.

Call it fate or destiny, but when I was asked to pick up x-rays from the prior hospital, as big as it was, the first person I ran into was the other doctor. I found that ironic considering the circumstances. I was limping and hobbling along with a crutch. He had written me off and lumped me into a statistic of other folks who would be forgotten. That's how I felt about him, abandoned, yet at the same time relieved that I was still living, walking, and breathing. (He had no idea that I had a dream.)

I raised my hand to greet him as I passed. He gave me a big smile and my first thought was that he had no idea who I was. For the brief seconds that our paths crossed, something seemed quite unnatural about him. Before, it had been as if he were a ghost and at that moment it seemed that way even more. I picked up the packet of my x-rays to take to my new appointment. That was to take place at an entirely separate hospital across town.

As I made my way out of the hospital I could feel that the doctor kept watching me. I could feel his eyes turning with my every move. I left the building thinking that for some reason I couldn't get out of there without being reminded of my previous experience.

The new doctor (the naturalist) had confidence in his skills. He went so far as to chide the other doctor as either being to old or outdated.

"I don't know this other doctor, but maybe his hands aren't fine tuned enough to do such a delicate procedure. I'll be doing this at a state of the art facility with the latest technology available and my own team of experts. I have every reason to believe it will be a complete success."

Although I still wasn't convinced, I proceeded with the surgery and as before had taken all the precautions, even fasting the night before. I awoke with a clean body and regular state of mind. There was nothing euphoric about it. I became one with the earth – hearing her tunes and my dancing in balance. It wasn't as if I were an ant marching off to the battlefield needing to fight for my life and never knowing if I'd return. I simply didn't worry about it.

My life as I knew it faded into the background as I was submerged into this new world of healing. My recovery would take months, although I really had no idea what the ultimate outcome would be.

The Hospital

My body was waking up as I was being wheeled from the recovery room. The surgery had happened and I was on my way to a specialized wing in the hospital. The last thing I remembered was a nice lady holding my hand saying that she was going to take care of me and then another gentlemen shoving her out the way saying that he was going to take over. The woman looked offended and puzzled as she hurried off. I was thinking before I had drifted off that this doctor really did bring his own team of experts.

The specialized ward was for orthopedic patients who were recovering from, back, spine, knee and hip injuries. It appeared to be run separately from the main hospital as the nurse stated.

"You're in a special place," she had said when I arrived.

The first set of nurses tended to me around the clock. They changed shifts every eight hours. A new nurse would arrive to take over just about the time I had gotten used to the other one. These nurses tended to my IV, and monitored my fluids and medication. It wasn't until the second day that I my head really cleared and I began noticing things. My body ached and was sore and swollen from the surgery. I couldn't feel half of my leg. The leg pumps that were hooked up to keep the blood flowing were similar to the ones I had before. There were tight white stockings with no toes squeezing my legs. I couldn't feel or move my toes. I was resigned to having to remain in one position (on my back). I could see the bandage stretching from my hip to my knee. It seemed to curve around and hit my buttock. Free lipo I thought. That's a bonus. I could barely move my body or my legs. There was a drainage tube leading from underneath the bandage. Bright red blood was seeping through a tube. I noticed that the nurses were coming to drain and catch the blood with a clear plastic cup. The cup was more than half full. How could I survive while losing so much blood I wondered.

"That's a lot of blood," I mentioned to the nurse.

She just looked at me not really paying attention. Another shift was changing and a nurse that I had before showed up.

"Did you change the bandage?" I heard her ask in low tones in the hall.

"Yes," the other nurse responded.

"Well why is this tube still here? It was supposed to be removed after 24 hours!"

"I didn't see any instructions for that," the other voice said.

"It's right here in plain sight! Can't you read!"

The nurse removed the tube talking under her breath to the other nurse as if she were incompetent. I knew that was too much blood to be losing.

Twenty four hours had passed and I was showing signs of stress. My daughters were present at my bed. I was talking to them and immediately started shivering and sweating profusely. I was talking out of my head they said and become delirious. I remember yelling and screaming at everybody for no reason. My temperature was dropping and people rushing around me were checking my vitals. I could feel myself losing consciousness. My voice sounded softer as I was slowly losing energy to move or speak.

"Maybe it's the medicine," I heard one of them say.

The IV was quickly detached from my arm. It was the right call. It was written in the charts as well as on the wristband I was wearing that I may be allergic to certain medicines. The morphine was causing a bad reaction. It was much worse that the "itch" attack I had at the other hospital. This time I thought I was going to die.

The nurses snapped me out of it and my mind gradually cleared. Everyone was relieved; I could tell by their faces. I think I had frightened the wits out of my young grandchild however, because she was too afraid to come back. It wasn't until Christmas that I saw her again.

The nurses monitored me more closely after that. The next day I was told that my blood count was too low. Ah, duh, I thought. If you lost that much blood your blood count would be low, too. I didn't say it out loud, of course.

"You're going to need a blood transfusion." the nurse said. "It would be too risky to wait for your blood volume to build back up on its own."

Sharing blood with another person had never crossed my mind before. But, if it could save my life, of course I would do it. I wondered why they couldn't use the blood that had drained from my body but was told that wasn't possible.

After receiving the new blood I felt revitalized. My energy was back and I had an appetite and was able to eat. The solid food diet they put me on was much better than the liquid. Previously, I had been so doped up food hadn't appealed to me. Things were going pretty standard I supposed aside from having been given the wrong medication, becoming delusional, and almost bleeding to death. I supposed that things could only get better from that point on.

My leg still wasn't responding and I began to become concerned about it. I asked if it was part of the normal recovery process. The physical therapist said no. I should have been able to move it by now or at least been be able to wiggle my toes.

I stared at the foot. It had an eerie resemblance to something I had seen before. It was long, square, weirdly stretched and meshed together. It looked like what I thought was the hand being pulled away in my dream. It had the exact shape and configuration. Maybe the dream was trying to tell me more than I thought. It gave me things to think about. Maybe the hand wasn't a hand at all. Perhaps it was a foot that was being taken away from me. My foot wouldn't move. It appeared to be paralyzed but I was told we wouldn't know until the swelling went down. A very strange feeling came over me – that there was a direct connection between the dream and what I was experiencing.

The physical therapist kept asking me what I had done to myself in the past. I told him absolutely nothing except try to recover from my injuries. I felt offended from the insinuation. Upon discovering that I couldn't walk, many of the nurses seemed taken, also. I felt on the offensive having to explain something that I thought the doctor should have taken care of.

"Just think," the PT said, "if this is the way your foot turned out from this doctor, imagine what could have happened had the other doctor gone through with it. You probably would have died."

Where had I heard that before, I wondered to myself. It had come from the kind doctor with the foreign accent that followed up with me in my room after the failed surgery. Upon reflection, it seemed the PT was telling me I should be grateful.

Where was my doctor? I needed to know what was going on. I had told him he should be very sure that he could do this successfully before I would consider proceeding. He had reassured me that he could.

Several other staff doctors had visited my room on a regular basis to ask me how I was doing. They found it surprising that my doctor hadn't been into see me yet. I was growing uneasy since drawing the correlation with the dream. I was hoping it wasn't true.

I had many questions when the doctor finally arrived.

"Is it true I have what's called foot drop?"

"I don't know," he said. "This is very strange and has never happened before. It could be that or something else. I'm puzzled as to why your whole appendage won't move. We were very careful and took every precaution. The surgery took longer than usual and the angle I had to use to make the incision was unusual making it more difficult. But I'm confident that we did everything we could and were as careful as possible not to make any mistakes. I'm not perfect, but I believe we did the very best that could be done."

My doctor didn't know it, but it was at that moment that I found complete confidence in him. He was an honest man and that was good enough for me. Even if my leg wasn't recovering, I somehow knew my fate was bigger than him or that moment. I sensed that it had not been entirely in his hands. I didn't blame him or put him at fault. I would except the consequences whatever they were to be.

He mentioned that I might have to go to a rehabilitation facility to recover. I accepted that. I continued to complain about the pain and the fact no one seemed to be doing anything to get that leg working again. Then it happened. The nurse from hell arrived.

The Nurse From Hell

Imagine being in your hospital bed in pain and unable to walk or do for yourself relying totally on nurses who were supposed to be experts with my sort of condition. I was grateful for their service don't get me wrong. I knew I couldn't have made it without them even though everything didn't always go smoothly.

But there was this one nurse that was evil cloaked in darkness. My mother had been a nurse by profession and before this experience, I admired the profession. I would never have guessed anything could turn that opinion around so completely. At first glance she seemed to have had a nice smile and a pleasant demeanor. But I had been fooled by several others the same way.

The male nurses were the worst. I'm not sure if they were just too embarrassed or they just didn't care and thought they could get away with shirking their responsibilities. One African nurse was visibly and verbally upset when she found the state I had been left in by one of them. She made it a point to wash me down and bathe me and make sure I was clean. I was grateful.

The holiday season neared, and I could see the faces of the staff changing again. I had worked in many jobs myself and knew that in most cases seniority ruled. Most people wanted the holidays off to be home with family. I had resigned myself to having to spend Christmas in the hospital. My kids hadn't been there to see me in awhile and I was looking forward to their visit.

On Christmas eve I woke up when a nurse came in to give me medicine. She was about to change shift with another nurse. I hadn't seen either of them before. She said she was going to give me my medication and handed me the concoction of pills in the little white cup. She explained each one as she handed it to me. When it came to the blood pressure medication she said it was 100 milligrams. I told her that dose was too high. She said she would check on it and in the meantime I could take half the dose. An oversight perhaps I thought. I hoped they hadn't been giving me the wrong dosage all that time. It turned out they *had* been, but this nurse had checked and then lowered the dose. I specifically overheard her tell the next nurse that I was to receive half a pill until my new pills with the correct dosage arrived.

I paid no more attention to it figuring it had been handled and glad I had had my wits about me earlier. I trusted that they would do the right thing.

Come evening, it was clear they were short handed. I spent the whole night with out having a nurse respond as I pushed the call button for assistance. She either ignored me on purpose or didn't hear it. What I do know is that it only happened on her shift. I became so frustrated that I simply stopped calling. When a new male orderly arrived I resigned myself to believing that between the two of them I'd be in pain and my needs would go unattended to. I tried to make it to the potty on my own when the man walked in.

"You never call for help do you?" he asked.

That was my first clue.

When she did come in she ignored my request to hook up the leg pumps that had been on my legs since surgery. She said that was somebody else's job and left. Again, it only happened on her shift. I wondered whose job it was and why the other nurses hadn't known it was somebody else's job. So I spent Christmas morning without my leg pumps.

Here are just a few of the things she managed to do: You be the judge: snatched off dressing hurtfully, gave wrong dosage deliberately, stormed into the room calling a doctor a kook, gave me the evil eye when I requested help and paced slowly around my bed as if to intimidate me, told me she had the power to send me home if I didn't behave, ignored the call button when I needed help, told me no one was available to help me, and more.

The Ambulance

I had never ridden in an ambulance before or been on that sort of gurney. The one I was on rose up and down and was narrow, just wide enough to slide into the small space available in the ambulance. It was a tight fit since I was really too large for it being swollen as I was from the medicine and period of inactivity .

"Don't they make these transports bigger," I asked.

The attendant's solution was to pull the straps tighter across my body. He had missed my point. I held a vase of flowers on my stomach. They had been brought by visitors and I so dearly appreciated them I wasn't going to leave them behind.

Really, I appreciated how kind the attendants were the entire trip. The small one drove while the larger one sat in back with me. I felt sandwiched like a sardine. I looked around and saw emergency equipment everywhere.

It was a ride I would never forget. I lay there strapped tight and unable to move holding a bouquet of flowers in my chest. It felt like I was practicing for my coffin debut. If I didn't make it, I thought, it was a most appropriate position from with to leave this world.

The attendant leaned in close, and began asking me questions. He looked awkward trying to wrestle with the piece of paper and writing board he held on his knee.

"Whats your age and date of birth?" he began.

"Don't you have all this information." I said, "Aren't you

carrying my records from the hospital?"

He must have been used to such protests because his manner remained kind and gracious.

"I just need to fill it out for my own form." he said, "We're required to do that. Insurance won't pay without it."

I complied, if reluctantly. He shortened the interview as a result.

The Nursing Home

Our approach to the nursing home was quiet and subdued. There were no sirens, since this was not an emergency, and there was no fan fare waiting to greet us.

These fellows knew exactly what they were doing and wheeled me directly to my room. They had clearly done it countless times. They placed my vase of flowers next to me on the nightstand and asked for my signature on the release form.

After they left, I immediately became aware of moans coming from the other side of the room. There was also some sort of mechanical sound – some kind of device running. Lots of folks were in and out of the room attending to whomever it was on the other side of the curtain that divided the room. There was no way I could see who it was. Presently, a young lady emerged from behind the curtain. She seemed both surprised I was there and happy to see me.

"Oh, good, a roommate!" she said pleasantly.

I was too weak to acknowledge her with words. I nodded and smiled. But I did sympathize with the lady on the other side because I was in need of help myself.

Confined to the bed and not able to move because of the pain, I tried to shift my body to get comfortable. There is no feeling so helpless as the feeling of wanting to move but being unable to. I was relieved on the one hand that I had left the hospital, but apprehensive about what I was getting into.

I had become desperate to leave that place so had high hopes for The Manor. It looked like a very nice facility from the outside. The grounds seemed peaceful and serene from what I could see as we had approached in the night.

As the night wore on, the nurses and orderlies were in and out of the room often, mostly to tend to my roommate. She apparently required round the clock care. Sometime during the night, the room heated up like a sauna and it became hard for me to breathe. I rang repeatedly for assistance.

"Can you turn the heat down or open a window?" I asked.

"I'm sorry but we can't do that. 'Mother', (as my roommate was called), needs the temperature up at night – her oxygen and all."

I had no idea what that meant other than that my request had been denied. I immediately asked for another room.

"They're all full," she said. "Maybe tomorrow. I'll put in your request with the head nurse."

There was a male attendant with an accent taking care of my roommate who he, also, affectionately called, mother. I asked if he could get me a potty chair?

"I'm not able to make it to the restroom by myself," I added.

"That's what we're here for," he said in what seemed to be a friendly manner. "Just tell me when you need my help."

"I'm telling you I have to go, now."

The staff at the facility didn't seem to understand my condition. It may not have been obvious to them that I couldn't move my leg and could barely move the rest of my body. I was much younger than most of the residents but I was sure there must have been others around my age. They seemed to define my abilities according to my age rather than by consulting my chart.

I felt helpless. The young man was small in stature and barely strong enough to get me into the wheelchair. After leaving me in the bathroom, he never returned. I had to call another assistant to help me get back to bed.

Another lady appeared when the shift changed. She was a petite and extremely thin woman with the same accent as the man. I took the opportunity to ask her for a larger potty chair than the one the gentleman had brought me. It was too cramped.

Apparently it was the only size they had as I never got another one.

I made it through the night. Things didn't improve during the next day. Noon came and went. Dinner time came and went. The staff had had been inattentive, to say the least.

With the middle of the night, the hot, humid, the sauna-like condition returned. The sounds of the old lady breathing with her oxygen tank seemed to get much louder at night. Tears welled up in my eyes. No one seemed to care about my discomfort. No one seemed to care about me. The helplessness I felt became frightening.

A nurse came into my room. I hadn't seen her before. Her face was expressionless as she went about her duties humorlessly, yet all quite efficiently.

"Ouch," I said as she tried moving my leg into another position.

Sensing she was hurting me she immediately corrected what she was doing. She had been the first nurse that hadn't complained when I expressed how I was feeling or what I needed.

The air and space I was breathing in didn't seem real. In the back of my mind, neither did the people surrounding me. I was beginning to think that this place was a figment of my imagination and that I had been transported back to another place and time. That was even supported by my vision of the very old building when I was wheeled inside for the first time.

If there were such a thing as a transposed moment, that would have been it.

The people and events were carrying out their duties in a robotic fashion as if they were either trapped in purgatory or elected to be there. Most everything about the place resembled an ancient, older, facility, the kind that existed long ago and merely lives on through its modern day name. The exterior, however, had seemed modern.

Mother's TV was always too loud when it was on and it was always on. I asked one of her helpers it he could turn it down. I needed to sleep.

"Mother is hard of hearing," the guy with the accent said, "but I'll see what I can do. He turned it down a notch – still way too loud – and he left the room.

I complained again to the next person that came in. They would swiftly move past and go directly to mother, ignoring me and my requests.

"I really can't sleep with the volume that loud and I'm tired and hurting," I called after the helper had moved behind the curtain.

The lady that had examined me upon arrival entered my room. She had looked and probed my private areas in ways that seemed fully inappropriate and unnecessary. Again, she pulled down the sheet and pulled up my gown, repeating that exam as if I were carrying fleas. I felt violated – for a second time – and could only protest as she searched between my legs. She offered a faint explanation when I complained.

"Some folks come in her with all kinds of stuff."

"Well, I'm not one of them," I said forcefully. "Didn't you read my chart?"

"No, that is for the nurses. We don't usually have access to it."

"Well, next time I suggest you do that before violating a near paralyzed woman."

Her shift was over and the male with the accent returned.

He ignored me twice as I asked him to get me a larger potty chair. He all quite deliberately walked past as if I had become quite a bother to him. He moved behind the curtain and tended to mother.

At shift change, he passed the buck to another lady, a tall thin lady with an accent similar to his.

"I'll try finding you one she said. Don't worry about it if it spills over, that's what we're here for to help you and clean it up."

She sounded nice enough – though an odd approach to patient care, I thought. She had a pleasant smile. There was something about her that was strange though. She eventually came back and built a makeshift potty. Not only was it too narrow for me to fit into, but the small bucket she had found to place underneath was too small and poorly positioned. I was puzzled that they were more willing to clean up a mess than provide the proper equipment in the first place.

The arrangement worked no better than I thought it would. I was already sad because I could not help myself, but to not have decent toilet accommodations was a travesty.

The woman returned and cleaned things up. She was so nice and sweet I couldn't be mad at her. I was more mad at the facility for the quality of care and equipment they were providing for me.

Not only was I feeling neglected, but I wanted to be left alone. If these assistants weren't going to tend to my needs in a wholesome way then what was I doing there? It made no sense.

"When will the doctor come to see me?" I asked.

"The doctor makes his rounds twice a month."

"What?" Surely My doctor is going to come before that! I am only scheduled to be here two weeks for rehab."

"You just missed him. He came on Monday so wont be back for two weeks."

"Is he the only doctor?" I asked.

"He's a facility doctor and there is no one else."

"I should be ready to go home by then. I really don't understand. How will he know if I'm ready to leave?"

"The nurse keeps regular contact and informs him of everything."

She could see how upset I was.

"You can contact your own doctor if you have an emergency but normally they don't see you until your follow up visit after you go home. I see that yours is scheduled in about 3 weeks."

That was fully unsatisfactory. I had an earful for somebody and apparently lots of time to rehearse it!

***

I could hear screams during the night from neighboring rooms. It was hard to describe them – hollow, perhaps. I hadn't been out of the room yet so didn't know what the inside of the facility looked like.

"What happened to my request to change rooms?" I asked the afternoon attendant.

The invasive lady had returned.

"I told the nurse and she said she's working on it."

The male aide walked out from behind the curtain. They greeted each other in their native language.

"Please turn down the volume on her TV. I am unable to sleep with it up so loud."

It was no secret. Even the aides had to raise their voices because of how loud the TV was. They both ignored me. I had had it! It was now approaching the evening and mother's TV was still blasting.

Both aides left the room.

How could they not comply with my wishes. I began to wonder if it was meant to torment me?

And what was all that about the room needing to be hot because of something to do with the oxygen tank she was hooked up to? It seemed that in order to help her breathe they were willing to impair my ability to breathe. It made no sense. The situation would be unbearable even for a person that wasn't sick!

I called my daughter.

"My roommate's television is too loud and they won't turn it down!"

"What?" My daughter asked.

"This room feels like a sauna and I'm suffocating! Nobody will help me."

"What? she asked again.

"They keep coming into the room but won't help me get on and off the potty chair! And they won't turn down the TV."

"What the hell!" she exclaimed.

I held my cell phone up so she could hear.

"See, I told you!" I said when I got back on the phone.

"Well, I'll call up there to see what's going on.'"

"No! Don't call. Come and get me! Right now! I want out of here."

I hung up.

The male assistant walked by again as if nothing was unusual.

"I want to go home! I told him."

"You can't go home. It's late at night and there's no one here to discharge you."

"I'm told that the doctor doesn't come for two weeks! I'm discharging myself!"

I started screaming.

"I'm leaving!"

"You can't!" he protested, clearly attempting to calm his tone and manner.

"You just watch me!"

I lifted my aching body into the wheelchair beside the bed and began wheeling myself over to the drawers and closet that had my things. It caused me terrible pain.

He left the room.

I called my daughter again and insisted that she pick me up immediately.

As I was throwing things into the bag, the nurse walked in.

"What's going on?" she asked.

The male aide had returned with her and was standing at her side.

"Don't you hear me!" I said tears rolling down my face. "I'm leaving! I just want to get some sleep. That's all I ask. I need sleep! If no one cares about me then I don't need to be here! I'm a patient too!"

I whirled around in the chair to face them directly.

"I have asked to be changed to another room multiple times. I haven't been. I've asked to have that television turned down but no one will do that. Could you sleep in here with the TV blasting away like that? That's it! I've had it. I'm going home!"

"How are you going home?" she asked.

"My daughter's coming to pick me up."

"How does your daughter know?"

"Because I talked to her!"

The nurse looked at the house phone on the night table next to the bed. She acted as if it would have been impossible for me to make a call.

"That phone hasn't been used all day," she said.

How did she know that? I wondered.

I flashed my cell phone.

"With this! She knows all about things here. While we talked I put the phone on speaker so she could hear how loud the TV is, too!"

The nurse looked stunned and no longer talked as if she had the upper hand.

"I'm sorry," she said. "I can get you another room right now. You don't have to leave."

"It's too late! I just want to go home!"

At that point I was crying like a helpless baby.

Someone came into the room and told the nurse she had a phone call. She left the room. It was my daughter calling to check up on me.

"What are you guys doing to my mother? Why is my mother calling me at 12:00 at night begging me to come get her? She is a strong woman and would never complain unless something is really going on!"

The nurse acted quickly to get me another room.

There's another room available but it costs more. Are you willing to pay the difference.

"No," I said. "I told you, I'm going home!"

She practically begged me to stay, at least for the rest of the night.

"You said you want to get some sleep. Why don't you at least stay for the night and then decide what you want to do in the morning."

I agreed in a huff. It had been a tiring, long, night. I wheeled myself down the hall and around the corner to an entirely separate wing, following the nurse. I went reluctantly and allowed no help. I left my things behind in the other room.

If all of this had taken place within the first two days of my being there, how could I possibly put up with two weeks.

I slept with one eye open. Although I was no longer sharing a room, I still didn't feel comfortable. The room was dark and for some reason scary. A strange man kept walking past the room rolling a cart. He had a hunched back. He appeared dark and mysterious although I couldn't see his face. I asked them to keep the door open. That night was very creepy.

I had survived the night. Even with the creepy man who I had visions of sneaking into my room and smothering me.

Bright and early the next morning, two pleasant people arrived in my room. The Occupational Therapist and the Physical Therapist. Each one introduced herself. Had it not been for those two individuals, my entire stay there would have been unbearable.

I was to have an appointment with each of them every day.

The Occupational Therapist was going to show me how to use gadgets (walker, grabber, shoe horn, etc.). The Physical Therapist was a jewel. She was very personable and said she requested me specifically. She said she wanted to work with me and scheduled all our appointments ahead of time.

Unlike the Physical Therapist I had at the hospital, she was very patient as well as inspiring. I looked forward to the sessions that we had even though there was always some pain involved.

I was moved to another room after spending my night of horror there alone and had a new roommate.

The robotic woman that had helped me in my other room arrived to help. Despite her stilted approach, she turned out to provide good service. I was amused by her mechanical manner. It was as if she didn't belong there. OR, maybe she did.

She spoke in a monotone and never looked me in the eye. She seemed to want to keep me comfortable and never flinched when I suggested ways of comforting me.

I had everything at stake: my health, my pain, my mental stability, and my recovery. She served me well in all those ways.

The physical therapy room gave me a ray of hope. I could open up to my physical therapist and talk to her.

"I don't think the doctor did this on purpose," I told her.

"What do you mean?" she asked.

"My leg, my foot. The people in the hospital were acting like I was going to sue or something and their only concern was protecting their interest. But suing is the furthest thing from my mind because I had faith in my doctor."

"How so?" she asked.

"Well, it was when he came to my room and sat on the hospital bed to see how I was doing. No one ever mentioned the term 'foot drop' except for the physical therapist and some nurse assistants. It was as if the nurses and doctor wanted to avoid saying it. So, when I asked the doctor if he thought I had 'foot drop' and if my leg would ever recover, he had been very honest. He said that he believed that was what it might be. He also said that his team had done their very best. He explained that he had to make a bigger incision than he wanted to, and the angle for the surgery was difficult and somewhat unusual. He said that he took his time to make sure things were done correctly.

"It was at that moment that I knew I was looking into the face of an honest man. He had done his very best. I believed him and that was good enough for me. It was I who would have to live with the decision I had made no matter what the consequences."

Could that have been what fueled the fire, I wondered, in retrospect. It did seem that the nurses had changed their approach with me once they got the updated status on my condition.

At any rate, I had no intention of suing the doctor. Now, if there were a way to sue the nurse from hell or the Manor for the way they treated me those first several day, I just might consider that.

The physical therapist agreed with me.

"Well I don't know this doctor," she said, "but if you believe that about him it probably is true. Doctors can only do their best, they don't deliberately try to maim us."

So it was a joy and delight to have her as my physical therapist and although she didn't know it she was my "mental therapist" as well.

My new roommate was a nice elderly lady. We hit it off the first time we met. How could two people who seemed so entirely different have so much in common. I was starting to believe she was put there specifically for me.

I believe that God puts people in your life for a reason. And while she said I was helping her, she was really helping me.

Our names sounded similar. Often we couldn't tell if the nurses were saying my last name or her first name. We both responded when we heard it. By putting an 'S' on the end of her first name, Joan could easily sound like my last name, Jones.

Several interesting similarities came out as we got to know each other.

We found out that we like the same shows. When I turned my TV to a channel, I'd find her watching the same channel on her TV. Whether it was politics, comedy or a news broadcast it seemed to be that way.

Although she was almost thirty years my senior, she acted like a spring chicken, full of life and enthusiasm. That's how my friends would have described me.

She had had surgery on the opposite hip from mine. But unlike the basis for my problem – arthritis – she had fallen and broken hers.

It was very easy to talk with her. We had lighthearted conversations and laughed at the same things. We talked to each other like friends who had known each other for a long time. I couldn't help but feel that if we had met somehow on the outside (which seemed highly unlikely) we would be the best of friends.

Her world seemed completely different from mine. She was an elderly white lady who was getting a second chance at marriage by reconnecting with her first husband. Her only daughter was suffering with cancer. She had two grandsons that she adored. One was soon to be married.

She told me I was a nice kind woman whom she felt she had known for a long time. She said that talking to me was easy and our friendship seemed to come naturally. I told her those feelings were mutual.

Given our age difference our bond wasn't like mother and daughter; it was like long lost friends. I couldn't get over the feeling that she had been placed there specifically to befriend me.

Upon first meeting her that first night, I had come to the room under duress. Not even sure if I wanted to stay, I was reluctant to meet another roommate especially someone that might be like mother. I never had to explain any of that. She seemed to understand how things could get. Even that first night she had a way of setting my mind at ease.

"They never come when I call," she said. "How about you or did you just get here?"

"No. I came from another room. And you're right; they don't respond when needed. I told her about the robotic woman that acted strange but was the most helpful. She hadn't had contact with her.

There were a string of new assistants on this wing of the floor. They too spoke with accents but it was Hispanic – more familiar to my ears. They were mostly pleasant but the same problems of promptness continued there.

"It's not easy having to depend on someone else," I said. "It's a lot harder right now but I'd still rather try it myself first."

"Well I cant, yet! She said. "I'm going to make them do their job!"

She pressed her button. There was no response. Twenty minutes later there had still been no response.

I felt so sorry for her. I pressed my button, too, hoping that if I could get someone to respond I would tell them about her.

Someone showed up. I tried for her on several different

occasions. Although it was a new person each time, we eventually figured out a system. We'd tag team, pressing the call button so that if someone showed up for one person we'd also send them over to the other.

It worked remarkably well! We soon had the aides eating out of our hands. We were being well fed and well taken care of. It became like a wonderful secret between the two us.

Besides my positive experiences with the two therapists, I was still disgusted with the place in general because none of the floor help seemed to know how to handle my leg properly and I still hadn't seen the doctor. I preferred to do things on my own so I mostly used the call button to help my roommate. If I needed to go to the toilet or wash up, I'd do it myself. I was showing more and more independence and believed I was ready to leave. If only the doctor would come so I could ask him for a discharge.

A doctor finally showed up. He went straight to my roommates curtain. I could hear him talking. Anticipating that he would see me next I listened in.

She wasn't satisfied with the answers he was giving her and could give her no idea when she would be ready to leave. She told him it was important for have some idea about her discharge date so she could arrange for help when she got home.

When it grew silent over there I called: "Doctor please, before you go, can I see you?"

He had already left.

"That was my personal doctor," she said. "He's not the facility doctor. I made a special request to see him. But, since he didn't tell me anything different than I already know, it was a waste of time and money."

I would just have to wait for the facility doctor. As long as my pain meds were coming and working, and I was able to rest, the other complaints seemed minor.

My children came to visit me several time during the first week. It was always nice to see them. My roommate's children came more often than mine. Even the daughter that knew she was dying of cancer came to visit. It turned out that she had been here before – in this same room and in the same bed even as her mother. We were reminded of that every time she came. Several of the aides would show up to say hello to her. She had beaten the odds so far by living as long as she had.

I had been settled in the room for a number of days when my roommate started having hallucinations.

"Maybe it's the medication," she said searching for a reason. "They keep changing my doses."

It reminded me of when I was in the hospital and had that bad medicine reaction.

"Maybe so," I agreed.

I noticed that each night her behavior became a little stranger than the night before.

Nights became in strange in another way, as well. We would hear a man calling out – fearful and confused.

"I wish someone would help him," I said. "Do you hear that?"

"Yes, I can hear it," she said quietly.

"This place feels like it's some kind of repeat in time – like it's been here before. I can't really explain it, but it's like there's something really strange about it. Some of the attendants seem like they've been transported here from another age."

We were talking through the curtains.

"I was feeling the same way," she said. "But I wasn't sure how to say it."

We both lay on our backs in silence listening to the ghostly sound of the person down the hall crying out for help.

I drifted off to sleep.

"Did you see that?"

I was awakened by Joan's question.

"See what?" I said startled from my sleep.

"The people coming through the walls! The walls were opening up and the people were reaching down to grab me. There was an odd energy present. The corners are still peeled back, can't you see it?"

I was wide awake by then. I checked out the ceiling and walls but I didn't see anything.

"What kind of energy was it?" I asked. "How do you feel about it?"

"They were speaking in Spanish. A man, was reaching down to grab me. Bad energy. It was Bad energy! I don't think I'm going to make it."

She started to cry.

"I don't think I'm ever going to go home. I think I'm going to die here."

"I don't want any part of it, I told her. I don't want any part of any negative energy. But you're not going to die."

I scanned the room again for any peeled back corners. She could still see them. I saw nothing.

Joan calmed down and presently I heard the heavy breathing of sleep coming from her side of the room.

It was the middle of the night and I was reluctant to fall back to sleep but somehow I did.

I was awakened again by an attendant who left Joan's area and came to mine. It was the robotic lady. She filled my glass in the same stiff manner she had almost a week before when I was in the other room.

She left.

"It's her!" I said to Joan. "The one I mentioned to you."

"She was strange, alright," she said. "She came in earlier, right before I had the dream about the peeled back walls."

"That's the one I was talking about. She doesn't belong with the rest of them. Its as if she's been here before like maybe a long time ago. In a different place and time."

"I was thinking the same thing," she said.

It was uncanny how we were both feeling the same way about the facility. I began to be able to sort through the impressions I had been having. It was as if the place were an old facility that had been transposed over another – a more modern place. It was as if they were occupying the same place and that there was some confusion in time. It was as if spirits were present and those spirits were in the form of some of the people we encountered.

Some specific examples came to mind.

There was the extremely thin woman that left me the bucket underneath the potty chair and although she tried to assist me wasn't able to help. I never saw her again. And the robotic woman who performs her duty diligently and efficiently with no feeling or emotion, it is as if she's programmed.

At that moment as I looked up, there was the hunch back man

I had seen walking the hall earlier. He was right there, standing over me, the dark sinister character whose face I had never seen. Oddly, I thought, he showed up at almost the same time as the robotic lady.

"May I get you something?" I heard a voice say.

Something compelled me to look up into his face. He gave me a nice smile. I smiled back. Then he disappeared and I never saw him again.

It had all happened at the time the place began to feel like it was occupying another time period – Joan had the dream and those two characters appeared. Coincidental or something else, I wondered!

I spent another night processing what Joan had gone through. I was growing weary and had a growing urge to go home. I was still having physical therapy every afternoon, but they changed therapists on me. We were both upset about it.

I saw that she was across the hall working with another person. When she left, she stuck her head in the door and told me that she had tried to change her schedule to include me, but they wouldn't let her. She was excellent at her job. She got me to walk forward taking baby steps. She adjusted the walker and the wheelchair to make them fit me. And when I grew tired she would wheel me back to my room. Each day she coaxed me to do just a little more than the day before. I couldn't have asked for anyone better.

"Don't rush it she said. It's going to take time to heal."

I saw her for the last time two days before I went home. She told me that my leg was crooked and was sliding outward. She wanted to help me adjust it. She had me stand in front of a mirror to watch. I didn't believe it at first and thought it might have been a result of the heavy boot (leg brace). She said it was a possibility but she had been giving me exercises to straighten it out.

She told me that it could take up to a year for a nerve to grow back and become fully functional.

"Within six months if you have feeling than that is a good sign."

She was telling me the truth, speaking very frankly. I respected her expertise and appreciated her honesty.

I had accepted the fact that I might not be able to walk again without a walker or a cane. During that final session together I noticed something different about her - something I hadn't seen before. I noticed that her fingernails were painted black and bitten down to the nub. Her right hand was disfigured or deformed. I could see its twisted shape beneath the long sleeve of the white smock she was wearing.

How could I have missed those things before? I couldn't have, of course. There were others in the room. Oddly, they all were also maimed. I didn't understand but a strange thought flashed across my mind. Maybe they had been injured before in a past life and had dedicated their life – or death – to working here.

It was clear that they belonged to a different place and time and maybe chose to work here. Maybe there was a penance that needed to be worked off, but I got the feeling that this was voluntary, that they were here willingly of their own free accord.

There were old spirits that lived and worked here. How many there were I didn't know. But the ones that came across my path were here to help me. And it showed in their caring ways.

The night before I was to leave, my children came to visit and I told them about the strangeness I felt. I didn't go into detail about what that meant. It was overwhelming and too much.

My early release came as a surprise even though I had been applying a lot of pressure to leave. The nurse on staff could have easily told me when she brought me my daily regimen of pills, but it was the assistant that gave me the word.

"So, you're going home tomorrow. Are you excited?"

"I am? I said.

Later, I asked the head nurse why she didn't tell me.

She said she hadn't seen it on the schedule.

I could tell Joan doubted the story. She knew how things worked there.

I was giddy with excitement and couldn't wait. The next day couldn't come fast enough. I called my daughter to tell her the news.

"Are you sure you're ready?" she asked. "You have a lot of help there and when you get home, who are you gonna have?"

"It doesn't matter," I said. "I'm out of here!"

That night I was awakened by a dream. I dreamed that I was back home (in my home town) going to a funeral. It didn't tell me who's funeral I was attending. I was standing with a crowd of people. They were all family. There were hundreds of us gathered to mourn the death of this person. We were lined up on the sidewalk waiting for limos to take us somewhere. It was like we weren't at the actual place where the funeral was to take place. I remember a lot of backs being turned to me and only a few faces stood out for me to see. I knew I was at my aunts house although it wasn't a house I was familiar with. Still, I knew somehow that it was hers. I also saw my cousin (her daughter) and she was talking to me. I don't remember the words but I felt her presence. I also felt the presence of her son (my cousin) at his mothers house although I didn't see him. People were lined up sitting down along a cement wall that was at the bottom of the stairs that led to the house. There were so many people around that I decided to climb the grassy slope that led up to the porch. It would allow me to skip the first set of stairs. I was making my way up the hill touching people on the shoulder that I passed and making jokes. I wanted to lighten the mood. I shouted, "DeDe!" every time I passed someone to get a laugh. My son was at the top of the stairs standing on the porch.

"Hurry up mom!" he was saying. "You're holding everybody up. Everybody's waiting for you!"

"I'm coming!" I said.

I reached the top and he opened the door for me. My son stood there as meticulously dressed as I had ever seen him before. He wore dark brown dress shoes, a dark brown colored leather jacket, and a camel vest over a collared shirt. He appeared sharp and crisp. His was the only face that I could see and he was the only one that interacted with me face to face.

"Mom, I hope you won't be offended by this." he said, "but can I borrow a dollar?"

"Sure son. That's no problem."

I entered the brightly lit house. I supposed that was so I could change clothes so we all could go to the funeral. The dream ended without really being finished.

I woke on the morning I was to leave the The Manor. I texted my daughter about the dream telling her that I was going to a funeral. I was very nervous and anxious about it. It was early but Joan already had visitors. I could hear her telling them about her dream, how the Spanish speaking man was reaching down to grab her and walls that peeled back.

The phone rang. It was my son.

"Hello mother," he said. "I have some bad news."

"What is it?' I asked.

"Our cousin died."

I almost dropped the phone, it was so hard to believe. I proceeded to tell him about the dream. The people on Joan's side of the room sat silently – listening.

When I hung up with my son I was overcome with disbelief.

He was the last person I'd seen in the dream and the first person I talked to in the morning. I felt that was not a coincidence. My dream was directly related to it all.

Someone had died in my family and I had dreamed about it the night before. I was even at this person's mother's house in my dream.

I didn't know how to process it. I was happy to be going home but deeply saddened by the chain of events. Another link had been broken and I felt it to the core of my being.

The irony of it all was that I had seen a crow a few days before in the courtyard of the facility when I was looking out the window. I figured they might be hanging around because lots of people may die there, considering that it's a nursing home where elderly people come and often never leave.

"I'm going to die!" I could hear Joan say.

She was telling her daughter.

"See, she had a dream! It was about me!"

"You're not going to die," I said to her as I pulled back the curtain that separated us. "That dream wasn't about you, it was about my cousin."

I washed up, got dressed and prepared my belongings to go home. I felt bad that I wasn't going to be able to tell the physical therapist that I wouldn't see her again. But somehow, I think she knew.

It was time to take my stitches out. The Japanese nurse that had been popping up occasionally and was on duty that morning seemed to be taking her time. When she arrived she told me a long story about her son. How he was a doctor and she was proud of him. Again it felt like I was talking to an old soul – someone who wanted to be there for a specific reason. She could have either been paying penance or homage to something that had been experienced in a past life.

My oldest daughter came to get me.

As she wheeled me past Joan, we stopped. I blew her kisses and she blew them back. We were like two kids that had become close friends and would really miss each other.

"Goodbye," I said. "God Bless you!"

She wished me the same. Then she paused and said.

"You better hurry up and get out of here before they change their mind."

She flicked the backs of her hands at me as if to say, Scat or

Shoo.

    We exchanged one last smile and I urged my daughter to hurry us on our way.

    I really did wish Joan well and knew I would miss her.

The Recovery

Being at home again just wasn't the same. My children had made it comfortable for me. I still needed a lot of rehab before it would be known if my leg would heal. After two more weeks of driving back and forth to another hospital for physical therapy, I slowly began to get better. Still, it would be months before my toes would move even a little bit. Eventually, I got the feeling back in my entire leg and foot as well as movement of the leg. I was so happy when I was able to take off the boot and foot brace I wanted to celebrate.

I tried to complete the exercises the physical therapist was teaching me. She saw that I had used electrical stem before and gave it a try. I told her how I would get feelings in my legs every time I used it. I was so appreciative that she had taken time to study my medical records. She said that some people don't think that treatment really works – but since you never know, why not try it.

She sounded like the other PT at the old souls facility – The Manor.

Looking back, I cant help but think it was the spirits at the old souls facility that put me on my path to recovery.

The dream I had prior to having the surgery showed me this outcome – but at the time I didn't see it. The hand that was pulling back was the shape of my paralyzed foot. I couldn't help but stare at it and see it that way.

I remember telling my daughter that while I was in the hospital.

When the hand was pulling back maybe it wasn't a hand. Maybe it was something telling me that my foot would be paralyzed – that my ability to walk would be taken away. That the cellophane was over my face is undeniable. And my breath was definitely being taken away. But the hand represented something else. It was telling about what was yet to come.

***

Old Souls exist among us. I'm convinced of that. But until I entered that facility I had never encountered one. I used to have theories that a person was reincarnated because after death you could see a baby that looked so much like the person that died. So much so, that I thought the person got a second chance and was reborn again. But that was just a theory. It may have been related to DNA. I had nothing concrete to prove it.

I got a new meaning of purgatory while I was at the Old Souls facility. I believe it was for people who were maimed, had received help, and wanted to give back. So they chose to transpose themselves there. I strongly imagine that those folks weren't on the payroll and that there was no record of them. That's how strongly I believe in what I experienced.

Sometimes I even think that Joan was transplanted there for me. After all, she was in the same room where her daughter had been when when had been given only a few months to live. She somehow beat the odds. Maybe those folks were also really dead and had come back to help folks because of the care they received, maybe they were grateful and wanted to give back.

They surely helped me.

Sometimes I tell myself that I'm going to revisit that place to see if those people are still there. Especially Joan. My daughters even thought about calling to check on her.

One part of me tells me not do it – that the mission is complete. And another part of me thinks maybe I should.

But then I think about what Joan said as I was leaving: "Get out-BEFORE they change their mind."

That was a powerful statement. I must take heed. Maybe it is not my place to revisit what has come to pass. What do I think I can change or impact by doing that? Not a darn thing. It happened for a reason. It is in my past. Now it is for me to move on to another season.

Signed: Grateful To Be Alive

CHAPTER SIX

Passing the Gift

I believe that after that experience my daughters have become more in tune with me. They are asking more questions. Even my granddaughters are showing promising signs of interest and awareness.

I could be driving down the street and my six year old grandchild (the one that had the dream about me in Germany) will say, "Hey grandma. There's a Crow!"

What made her talk about them so calmly or matter of fact is beyond me. I think they are comfortable with them because of what they mean to me.

One of my oldest daughters has been on a soul searching quest. I try to give her open ended questions so as not to cloud her mind with too much information. By staying open maybe she will be more receptive to information. By thinking and believing only one way, I believe a person cuts himself off from wonderful possibilities.

This is the same daughter that watched every episode of Super Soul Sunday and Life Class. This is also the daughter that has understood what it meant every time I mentioned to her about the crows.

The story I haven't told her is about the crows that lined up between here and her house on the day she lost the baby, or the silhouette I saw of her fiance who sat there sad with his head in his hands at the top of stairs.

Perhaps she will read this one day and think about all the signs I told her about leading up to it, but not knowing it was she.

I have a lot to tell my kids, much of which they've come to know in some form or another, bits and pieces. I need to fill in the details for them.

I have been the type of parent that leads by example. If I can tell you its hot you better believe it, by telling you that I've gotten burned may hit a little closer to home. I am not the type of parent that wants a child to go out there and have to get burned to learn that fire means fire.

Over time I have become more comfortable telling about my dreams. My children have come to understand that when their mother 'sees' something it must have merit. They seem satisfied with the bits and pieces and never delve deeply into on their own.

I'm still processing it all myself so I can understand their reluctance. I told my daughter not long ago that mine is a never ending story. As soon as I cross one bridge, there appears to be another waiting. That's why this book is cumulative and has been written over many years. It has been an evolving process that takes time to digest and organize.

And whenever I do get the answer to one of my questions - such as, why me -I've usually opened up the door to a whole other set of questions and answers. There's a hierarchy of knowledge and it comes in an order. It may not come when you need it but it comes when you are ready. Just as a flickering light can fade out so to can it allow its brilliance to shine when it's lit up again.

All knowledge is cumulative. So is feeding the soul. It has to be done consistently and constantly over time. Baby steps are necessary for all growth. In order to see how one thing applies to another we must piece it together. When we do that, we find that there is more in common than differences. It actually depends on where you place your focus and how you see things. Will you see them in a vacuum where they're closed off from society, or can you approach it as an open book trying to absorb and soak up all the knowledge that you can? The body is resilient. It will usually spit out that which is not good for us. So it may take time for us to see that we expel that which doesn't nourish us.

Yes, I try to teach my children to be an open book, that all knowledge it relevant whether good or bad. But relevant doesn't necessarily mean useful. There are somethings that don't ever need to known. And that is knowledge that can harm us. That stunts our growth and dims our light.

I have come to approach things as a blank slate. A pure strip of white lit up only by the brightness that shows its path. This is what I've come to know. This is the gift I've come to have and pass on to my children.

The Gift

Hindsight is 20/20 and just like my dreams, clarity is given once they, too, have come to pass.

My daughters tell me parts of their dreams. Some of them even include the crows.

I would tell my daughters, I don't know what another person's medium is, but I'm sure that everyone has one. It is a gift that only they can recognize and manifest over time.

I told them they may understand my dreams I tell to them but their medium may not be the same as mine.

God may have sent them another way of exploring and discovering truth. But, through DNA or through something else, I do believe that in some form, I have passed on my gift.

When they tell me their dreams I find myself listening to them only half-way because it will take something profound for me to notice a pattern over time. And maybe I may not be their safe-keeper - the one that should be privy to their sacred trust. Only they will be able to recognize that, the way I have come to recognize mine.

Maybe my reaction is nonchalant because it is normal to react that way. Or maybe I hear only what I want to hear. But I do know that I am paying attention. And when I hear something that gives me a sign, I will let that be known.

I believe everyone has inherited the gift in some way (my kids) some more than others.

Like I said, yours may come to you in a completely different way. It may not be the Crows or the Dreams. But, I guarantee you I will want to know what your medium is if and when you discover it. And even if you don't, just knowing that there is one is knowledge in itself. The prophets of every religion had insights far beyond the average man. Yet their insight was meant for everyday use. We can learn from them to see that God speaks to us. And for different people it might come in different ways. But discovering the meaning is our path – the meaning of what God has in store for us, whether its through a medium or in some other way.

Being closer to death has taught me more how to appreciate life. It has taught me that time is all we have when it comes to this world. And the essence of time is what will remain in us. For we are predated individuals with time stamps on our forehead. And we will be gathered together in the end in a shape and form with which we are familiar.

How do I know this? Because I have seen it.

Through the Clearness that is transposed over all of us.

The other world that exists and that will be calling us is full of people we know.

I heard them talking and being concerned, having a meeting about whether or not to take me. "Should we take her?" the voice asked.

I wasn't ready to go. Not that it's up to me but I stopped asking the question when I knew that if I were given the answer I would not be able to come back and tell you about it. No one has. I suppose, no one will. That is a fact of life – that the clearness is to remain separated until the time comes for you to know the answers. Then and only then will there be no turning back.

The Death Stalker

(Snatcher)

The Death Stalker came to me as I was awakening from a dream. It appeared to me in the form of a small tan creature with a pointed, cone shaped, top. There were no other features decipherable except that it wasn't the same shape or form in which I existed. It was standing upright, however. Why do I tell you this?

Because starting as a dream, it was every bit as disturbing as it sounds. Only I wasn't scared.

The creature told me that it was the Ogre of Death. It said, "I come to take people out of the equation."

I asked it, "Well, don't you have feelings? What about the babies? I repeated this twice asking specifically about the babies and children. How can someone (a baby) be smashed or squashed with blood and guts hanging out? Isn't that cruel?"

"But I don't have feelings," the creature said in a matter of fact manner. "I don't feel. I'm just doing my job. I'm just doing, what I'm supposed to do."

When I had this dream my sixteen year old granddaughter was spending the night. I had to tell someone. She was the closest person around.

I also told two of my other daughters the next day at their homes.

My daughters were more inquisitive about what the Ogre of Death said. I told them I called it the Death Stalker because it stalks people for death and snatches them out of the equation. The creature called itself the Ogre of death. I told them it's not for me to interpret, only to pass on what it said when it came to me in my dream.

A few days later I got the news. My mothers' brother had died. And like my cousin that died when I was in the nursing home, I was still recovering from my surgery and couldn't travel to the funeral. Maybe that's why I was going to a funeral in my dream at the nursing home because it felt like I had already been there.

Once the dream of the Ogre was off my chest I forgot about it. So, when the news came of my uncle's death, I really didn't immediately make the connection.

My daughter made a statement as we were riding in the car.

"I don't think I's over, do you?" It feels like something else is about to happen. I've been seeing a lot of crows."

We were dropping her son off at school. Her fiance heard the comment and looked as if he wanted to say something but was holding back.

I was still driving. I stopped at the stop sign before turning.

A very large crow plopped down right in front of my car. There were no other cars or people present – just the three of us riding in the car.

"Wow! I said, That crow is as large as the one I saw in Germany. It seems that ever since I left Germany I've been seeing larger crows than I did before.

"Maybe the one from Germany followed you home. Maybe it came all this way to tell you something."

"I don't know, but I'm sure going to say something to this crow!"

The crow had flown up above us and landed on a low roof. I backed the car up to say something to the crow.

"I know you're trying to tell me something," I said. "I just wanted to ask you, what?"

The Crow started cawing real loudly to the other birds.

"That crow is telling everybody," my daughter said. "Are you sure you were supposed to say something?"

"I'm not sure," I said, "but I had to. It landed on the street right in front of me. I just want to know."

Sonny had had enough. He couldn't hold back anymore.

"All this talk about birds!" He said. "And crows! Just because they're Black! That's superstitious!"

My daughter started arguing with him.

I told her not to argue about it. I said that the medium or the

Gift was not for everyone to understand. I said that everyone's not going to understand why we talk this way about the crows.

I said, "Why do you think I don't go around telling everybody?"

I told her ,"He doesn't know about the dreams that I've had through the years. He doesn't know about my journal in which I've logged everything and that I am writing a book. I respect his opinion because he has a valid point."

Sonny was relieved when I didn't shoot him down. I could see it in his face. But his frustration and disbelief was still there.

"I can have you guys talk to this man," he said. "He knows a lot about that stuff. Why can't you guys say this about another bird like a dove, why does it have to be the crows? Because its black, that's why. Crows don't mean sickness or death like you guys are trying to say. Ya'll are just superstitious!"

I told him I didn't know anything about the other birds; I only knew my relationship with the crows. I said I also understood where he was coming from and I held no ill feelings about it.

"You're saying everything associated with black is said to be bad. I agree with you."

Then I gave the example of how the term "Blackmail" is meant to mean something bad, but he's a 'black male'.

"That's not what this is. I told you this is something way deeper than that and has been going on for years. And I don't know what the crows mean to other people. I only know what they mean to me. Just like the one back there; it usually represents sickness or death. But I haven't had any dreams lately, so hopefully it doesn't mean anything. Usually, if there is death, I have a dream, too."

My daughter tried interjecting something in my defense. I hushed her up.

"It's not meant to be argued." I told her. "It's simply a fact."

I was proud that she was defending me. It meant that she really understood. But I was disturbed by her saying that she doesn't think it was over. I was also bothered that the crow showed up that way.

After dropping off her fiance, I drove my daughter to work. On the way back I got a phone call while driving on the freeway. It was my sister from back home. I put her on speaker phone and told her I'd have to talk to her while driving unless she could wait until I called her back when I got home. She blurted out what was on her mind:

"Your niece is taking her son off of life support!"

"What!"

I almost dropped the phone. I pulled into the parking lot at my place. I was shocked at the news. I was too sad to talk to anyone. I walked into the house and my granddaughter was there.

"Grandma who died?" she asked.

"Your cousin. He's a child. He is younger than you."

We hugged each other.

"We just saw the crow, too."

I told her what had just happened with the crow.

"But I didn't have a dream," I said talking under my breath.

I told her that unless I had a dream I wasn't gonna worry as much.

"But Grandma," she said. "You DID have a dream!"

'What dream did I have?" I asked.

"The one about the Ogre that snatches people. You said he comes to take people out of the equation."

"The Death Stalker," I replied.

I recalled the exchange and the part about taking children. And now, it seemed he had taken my nephew.

I was exasperated! I was speechless and had no more to say.

I found that I couldn't really let it go. I picked up my cell phone and called my daughters fiance.

"For the record, I began, you don't have to say anything, just listen. About those crows you were saying all that stuff about. I just want you to know that my nephew died."

Then I hung up.

I called my daughter. I reminded her of what she said about it not being over. She was shocked and hurt but she still didn't think it was over. I only halfway listened to her because I didn't want that to be true.

The next day my sister called reminding me that my uncle's funeral had occurred that weekend.

"It was on Saturday," she said. "Everyone that had flown in has left and returned home."

The funeral had been held at home where it happened. It wasn't all the news, however.

"There is more."

"What?" I asked her.

"Another cousin of ours has died. He was killed the day he arrived home from the uncle's funeral."

Thoughts raced through my head. It was too much to bear.

First, my uncle (my mother's brother), then her great grandson (my nephew), and now her nephew (my cousin). It had been uncle, nephew, cousin, in that order.

The death stalker (Ogre of death) had made good on what it said. It had snatched three of my people out of the equation. I had given it the name, Death Stalker, because I got the impression it did sweeping deaths – that it stalked for multiple deaths – the way it had that time.

It was True! It was just like my daughter had said. It hadn't been over. Even after the death of three of my relatives! The Crows were still around making their presence known. It had only been a week since my nephew's funeral.

My oldest daughter called me. Her dearest, dearest friend who was also a friend of the family had died. She was devastated and so was I to hear of yet another death that soon. We had been talking about visiting her recently but hadn't made any specific plans. It was a missed opportunity to perhaps spend time with her or say goodbye. We knew she had been battling cancer like my uncle but thought she was doing much better. The crows had hung around. I noticed them. And my two daughters noticed them. What we didn't know was that she had died that weekend following the deaths of my other loved ones.

The death stalker had come to claim one more life, but that time it was my daughter who had caught on to it.

…

Chapter 7:

Its hard To know What The Future Holds

You all say you're afraid of Death

The truth is...you're afraid of Life.

Fear comes from the unknown.

From guessing what it may be like

from day to day, hour to hour,

minute to minute.

Death doesn't stalk us,

It takes us at the opportune time.

I'm going to cry now

It is through the tears I shed that

I am relieved.

If we believe that the Joy

is yet to come

and that our pain and suffering

is to earn our credentials

for our passage…

Then we have yet to realize

That death is not a stalker

It is a natural phenomenon

Of the Life and death Process.

A Turn Of Events

My daughter was at my house visiting and watching me type at the computer when a strange feeling overtook me and I turned in her direction.

"I don't feel right. My heart is racing fast and it feels as if I might faint! It almost feels as if I'm not supposed to tell anybody about it."

"Maybe you should stop typing," she said.

"I don't know," I replied. "But it feels like something is preventing me, maybe trying to make me stop making key strokes. I'm a little scared and worried."

I tried to calm myself.

"Maybe this story isn't suppose to be out there."

I then retracted that.

"No, it is meant to be."

She said I should think about it. I tried to brush it off as normal anxiety from being excited about completing a project. This is the daughter that has been my closest ally on this journey, especially during recent events.

That night I went to sleep. All was quiet. I woke up slowly and sat on the edge of my bed and hesitated before I rose. I turned the light on, which was close to my bed. Suddenly, I became anxious, sweaty, and nervous while still sitting there. My heart was racing as if I could have a heart attack. It was the similar to the feeling I had while sitting at the computer, but more intense. I wondered to myself if the two were related. Why was this happening now, I wondered? Moments later, I witnessed a swizzle and a stirring of the clearness that was in front of me. It seemed the atmosphere became thick and was swirling around in front of me. I could see nothing but sensed rapid movement. Then I heard a voice. It was high pitch like a cartoon character's voice or maybe it sounded that way because it was moving so fast stirring up the atmosphere. It spoke.

"I should just kill her!"

I was stunned and sat there, frozen.

"Now I won't be able to spin around fast in my circles."

The being that was speaking was clearly angry. Angry at me! I surmised that it was related to finishing my book and talking about publishing it. It was the first time I was actually scared, really scared, for the moment. It was the first time a direct threat had been made on my life. When the entities before in the dream had asked, "Should we take her?" it was different and within a different context. I didn't feel threatened, then. I felt as if I had thwarted death. But this time something was wanting to kill me and it seemed personal! It was over nearly as soon as it had started.

That immediately turned my thoughts to the Ogre of Death that had showed up earlier in that very room (my bedroom). I wasn't sure how to take it. Thank God, that the feeling passed, once I shared it with my children.

So, I am not sure what it all means. It now seems as if a new and different element is present. I had never before in all these years of having dreams and seeing crows, had direct contact like that with another Being, for wont of a better term. I am convinced that there are others who can interact with us of their choosing. God is present among them. Based on the conversations to which I have been privy, they still ask permission or seek concurrence for what they propose to do.

I am still processing it all. I think and feel differently about life as a result of this. However, real fear has subsided as I come to better understand our exit from life. I also think that these entities feel that their secret is safe since they are separated from us.

IHSAN JONES

END OF BOOK

WHEN CROWS CALL

APPENDIX

Below is the Chronological list of events and dreams as I have recorded them and my thoughts about each one.

<u>My Dreams</u>

These are my dreams as they occurred and The Certain (strange) events surrounding them are also included:

The Crows

Communicating with the birds was a slow process. For me it seemed a life time. The mental telepathy that took place was more about interpretation than anything else. I was never good at reading bird body language or deciphering bird talk. I couldn't even distinguish one black bird from another. Their shimmering shiny black feathers were all I could make out. Oh, and the piercing black eyes. It was obvious how this bird got its name.

Historically associated with something mystical, the black bird has earned its reputation. These birds were known for dark magic and bad luck. I, like so many others, had given into the fables. In stark contrast to the black bird is the dove. Known for clarity and purity, I have no knowledge of what powers this one might possess. I do however, have a relationship with the crow.

My first encounter was in my teens. They started to appear in succession. Upon noticing that the birds were consistently showing up, I realized that they were trying to tell me something. I didn't know what that was.

Seeing only crows could mean sickness, illness or harm. But crows along with a dream meant death!

The Dreams

Along with the crows I would have dreams. They'd come in pairs: the crows, the dreams. This was my way of knowing the seriousness of the situation.

My dreams turned into nightmares with death staring me in

the face. Who's death and under what circumstances was always at question. My dreams never happened the way I saw them, They were always figurative. There was always a stand-in (character) playing the part of the real victim. Soon it wasn't hard to figure out. I knew that whoever died would, however, bare a likeness to the person(s) in my dream.

Trying to relive my dream was like trying to re-write history. You simply couldn't do it. Well, you could but it would be a lie. I'd try to change the script over and over hoping for a better outcome. Keeping my eyes closed a little longer and pretending to still be asleep simply would not work. I usually was so jittery after a nightmare that falling back to sleep was never an option.

The dual effects of the birds appearance and my dreams were a powerful force. Something special was taking place. No matter how unwanted it was. I felt different. Different from others. I isolated myself for protection, vowing to tell no one but trusted souls.

Dream #4 My Father

My father was ill. He had been that way since he retired from his job. He spent many days wrestling with his wheel chair. He never seemed to grasp the fact that he was in it permanently. Daddy was a hard man. What I mean by that is he was strong willed and of purpose. He worked hard most of his life to take care of his children. He stood close by my mother in support of raising them. After each dream I would experience the shakes, the spells, and intense feeling of loneliness and despair. Feelings that heightened and intensified as the time drew near. A dark cloud of suspicion hovered around me. I was curious yet not wanting to know. Oh, how I never wanted to carry this heavy burden. Thank goodness for my mother.

I came from a large family. My siblings and I were close. We were raised that way. Whatever went on in the family stayed in the family. It kind of reminded me of Vegas. And we had just as much drama, too.

What separated us and made us stand out is that we were close knit. My father was our protector. He stood over six feet tall and no one messed with him. He was well respected in our communities.

I loved my father and was very close to him. As a little girl it was easy for me to rest my head on his shoulder or get rubbed across my head with his palm. He was an affectionate man.

Both my parents had southern charm. They displayed it in everything they did. Mama wouldn't let her guests leave without sharing a meal. And Daddy made sure the food on our table was fresh from his garden. He cooked almost as well as my mom. His famous concoctions were drummed up straight out of the south; real pork rinds in "cracklin" corn bread, he put the "stringed" in his succulent corn beef and cabbage and the tender meat fell from the bone. Ripening tomatoes lined the kitchen windows and fresh picked mustard greens filled the kitchen sink. The aromas of the garden were prevalent in the kitchen but the smell of sweet purple plums and little green apples from the trees that Daddy had planted when we first moved there seemed to always be present. The huge squirrels that scuttled across the rooftop were well fed and had become a part of our family. These are the reasons I think that the crows were akin to me. They followed me wherever I'd go without me being aware. It took a good deal of time to discover this pattern.

I was very close to my father. When he died my whole world turned upside down. Of his nine children he let me know I was one of his favorites. I felt special growing up and knew I was loved. Daddy had been sick for a long time after retiring from his job. He had gotten a skin disease that progressed enough to leave him in a wheel chair. He got around that way for awhile with little assistance. Then his ailment worsened and his leg was amputated. Once that happened everything changed. Daddy was no longer the cordial man he had been. He'd rather be left alone than helped out by anyone. The medicines he was taking were more than you could count and he sat in that bed twenty four seven looking lonely. He had plenty of family to visit him, a television, radio and vcr, but Daddy chose to be left alone at most times.

Maybe it was because his room was cluttered with hospital equipment and it was impossible to move around. Or maybe because it was increasingly hard for him to accept the fact that a strong six foot five man had been reduced to a fragile old man needing lots of help. I loved my dad very much and I wouldn't have considered it a sacrifice to be there for him in his time of need. But the fact of the matter was that I lived 700 miles away and he had plenty of help. I did make a point of visiting my dad as often as I could. When I was there we'd laugh and talk even though you could smell sickness in the room. I don't think any senior citizen should be ashamed of wearing diapers considering they changed yours. But I also understood his feelings. I don't know what I would do in the same situation.

Daddy became bedridden and the nurses were tending to him three times a week. My mother picked up where they left off. My mother was a nurse by trade so caring for him in this manner was familiar territory. We found out later that Mesothelioma was a common disease for people that worked in his trade. He was a ship yard foreman and had been exposed to asbestos and lead for many years. Knowing that disease was a form of cancer we prepared ourselves for the worse. My Daddy lived until the age of 71 after retiring at 65. He died right before his 72nd birthday.

When Daddy went to the hospital we laughed. Most of his care was given at home so we knew he would give the hospital staff a hard time. He demanded and commanded them around like the sergeant in the army he once had been. We laughed because we knew he did this at home too. The nurses would all shuffle around catering to Mr. Jones. They'd act as if they were offended by his demands. But really they were used to it and it had become a joke around the hospital.

But the last time Daddy went to the hospital he never came home. We gathered there like it was the last day on earth. And for him it was. Amidst all the confusion as to whether or not we should resuscitate him if he needed it, half of us gave up and half of us didn't. it was comforting to see so many of his children and family gathered around his bed. You could see his face light up even though he couldn't speak. I held my father's hand almost to the end. I felt him squeeze it on occasion even when they said he couldn't. The tear in his eye let me know he wasn't quite ready to go but knew it was time. It was the only farewell I've had that was that overwhelming.

I couldn't cry because of the numbing medicine the doctor had put me on. The prescription pills were working long enough to hold back the tears. I had a story I held inside that no one knew about. It was about the events that preceded Daddy's death.

Even though the crows were keeping close tabs on me by being in my driveway and on my front lawn, there was on incident that really caught my attention. My daughter and I were traveling to the store. When we drove into the parking lot I saw a parking space. I didn't think that I was in competition to get it but soon found out that I was. I didn't see the lady in the car as she drove really fast to beat me to it. It wasn't serious enough for me to care or make a fuss about. I was sure I could find another. I continued to drive slowly heading past her as she exited her car. I had just mentioned to my daughter that there were lots of crows around minutes before. We had discussed that they were showing up because of Daddy. But beside the black birds that were in the parking lot there were also pigeons. The lady that stole the parking space walked past a pigeon and shooed it. She swung her purse and kicked at it in a harsh manner. What I saw next practically floored me.

A large black bird swooped down in front of her pecking her on the head and causing her to fall. She fell hard enough to end up with blood gushing from her head. She sat up for a moment as if she were dazed. People exiting the store saw her and offered to help. The lady then rose as quickly as she had fallen. It was amazing that she wasn't dead. She walked back to her car holding a tissue to her head. By the time I had reached a free space I no longer wanted to park let alone get out. I wasn't scared of the birds but knew this was something strange. The birds were trying to tell me something and she had interfered. It had been a succession of appearances and this was one of them. My daughter and I both sat with our mouths open. The bird was obviously defending the helpless pigeon that was hurt by the lady. The pigeon was eating food off the ground so the lady had clearly gone out of her way to do what she had done. Something like this only happened in the movies I thought. The lady could have been killed. And what would the witnesses say," that it was a bird! I suppose that was a striking moment for her – literally. She will think twice before ever shooing another pigeon. Although the moment was shocking I couldn't help but feel sorry for the lady. She could have died.

In Portland: My sister from southern California had to travel further than I to see my dad. Her husband needed to turn around because he had to take care of something back home. Daddy was sick and possibly would not make it. She turned to me and asked me if she thought they could make it back in time. Why she asked me I don't know. Maybe because I was standing the closest to her. Maybe because she felt a little guilty about leaving. I happened to glance up as we were chatting and saw on the telephone wire above a long line of crows that were gathering overhead. This was unusual and we hadn't noticed it before. It had to be clearly, hundreds of them. I turned and said:

"I don't think so. I don't think you'll make it back in time."

"Why do you say that she asked?"

I don't know, Sis, but there are a lot of crows over our heads gathering on the wire in front of our parent's house."

She turned to her husband and relayed my comment.

"She said we won't make it because of the crows. They both looked up and at that moment decided to stay. There was no more said about it.

A Vision that occurred (regarding my daughter)

Each time they come it is with a purpose. They bring a message that is generally about the sick, the ill, or the dying. I have never to this day gotten a message about something happy. That day was no exception. It was a Sunday and the beginning of the week. I had envisioned what was happening and didn't know it. Always a precursor to an event, these birds had finally tipped the scales. On this day, I saw things in the daytime instead of as they usually would come in the night. Had I been spared the details as the sun shone brightly? The birds were certainly there, following me as usual. Had the awkward birds chosen a newer venue? A day dream perhaps? I would soon find out.

I walked with a swift step as I left outside the back door of my house. I had to cross the playground, move through the parking lot and walk up a small flight of stairs to reach my destination – all the while anticipating that my daughter would be home. I needed to check on her. Felt compelled to do so. It was not normal for me to make the trek across the yard to get to her house. It was easier for me to jump into my black SUV and drive around the corner. That certainly could have spared me some steps.

Following instinct and running on adrenaline I decided to walk. Exiting my back door, which faced her house, I made my way in her direction. I caught a glimpse of crows. They were on the playground. No kids were playing. They were also landing in the parking lot and on the small strips of grass that made up the landscape. The patches of pink roses and blue and purple flowers that I admired were in clear view. Blackbirds were nestled among them. I had to pass them to get to the stairs. Although there were only a few, I still took notice. As I climbed the stairs I had a vision. It was a vision of my son in law sitting at the top of the stairs. He was holding his face in a sullen manner. No more details emerged, other than this shadowy illusion. Leaning forward with elbows propped on his knees he had the look of a worried man. I could feel the sadness even though no clouds were in the sky. I glanced back at the birds who were below me. I continued to climb. No comment, I said to myself. Do not say a word. I proceeded up the stairs. For although I had become familiar with their presence, I hadn't yet established a formal method of communication. It was wishful thinking. I must have walked directly thorough that shadowy figure because as soon as I got to the top I thought no more about it. It came and went just like the birds. Upon entering my daughter's house I found her pleasantly surprised. She was having a baby and was very excited. It took her and her husband a little while to wrap around the idea that this was happening.

An addition to their cozy clan was received lukewarm at first. Her two boys were enough to keep up with, she'd always say. This one was unexpected. I engaged her in small talk about how she was doing. She was glowing in the moment and rubbing her belly. I have a doctor's appointment coming up. Good I said. I can't wait to find out if it's a girl or boy. She agreed. I left after giving her a hug. Backtracking the same way as I arrived, I couldn't help but view one last image while at the bottom of the stairs. I raised my hand as if in a salute covering my eyebrows. I peered up but the sun was too bright. The image was again affixed at the top of the stairs. It was as if it belonged.

I HAD to say something that time as I passed the birds. They were trying to tell me something for sure and it was TOO obvious.

"OK, OK , I said in a frustrated manner, I get it!"

I may have even spoken loudly. Luckily for me, no one was outside.

The strangeness of the situation stayed with me. It was later that I would find out what it was.

I went about my business as usual, that week spending time shuffling kids back and forth to school and their various activities. I must have driven by those same stairs a dozen more times. One of those times, I actually saw Sonny sitting on the stairs in the same manner as in the vision. I glanced and thought no more of it. That Friday my daughter called me. I could hear the sadness in her voice. What's wrong? I asked. She hesitated. The baby had died.

Dream 5 (another nephew)

At the time of my nephew's death I didn't know which way to turn. I had been running about confused all day. I had a jittery feeling that something was about to happen. Crows were on the prowl. It had been awhile since I'd spoken to either of my boys and I was worried about them.

The dream started as jitters through the night. I attempted to go to bed but was restless and uneasy. Something just didn't feel right. I felt nervous and had the shakes. I sat at the edge of the bed and called my sons. They both who said they were okay.

I kept my bedroom door open so I could see throughout the house. My daughter's bedroom was directly across the hall and I could see her lying in bed. I told her I needed to talk to her brothers because of the feeling I had. I picked up the phone to speak with my boys. Just hearing their voice would have soothed me. I spoke to one of them but don't remember the details of the conversation. I do remember telling him I was worried and had anxiety. I often worried about my boys because they resided in another state. Because they lived so far away, I always had a feeling in the back of my mind that something could happen to any of them at anytime.

On that night I was alone in the house except for my youngest daughter. She had gone on to sleep but knew I was worried. That night after I had finally drifted off, I was awakened by a nightmare.

I had heard someone crying out for help. Their voice was faint. They were asking, over and over again, for someone to help them. It seemed like there was some type of discord in the background. I woke up feeling like someone had died and experienced an extreme bout of the shakes. I made phone calls to see if everything was okay back home. Mama had said her phone had rung in the middle of the night. She said she had answered it but couldn't make out the voice so she hung up. The phone rang again but went to voice mail. At 70 years old, my mother wasn't technology savvy enough to retrieve her voice mails. I had called my mother first thing in the morning but someone had been calling her in the wee hours. It was my nephew. Later that day I received devastating news. He had died.

My Mother

My mother's death caught me off guard. I wasn't prepared for her passing. If I had known about her suffering ahead of time I would easily have begged God to let me take her place. Although knowing mama, she wouldn't have it. I knew exactly what she would say in her quiet way.

"The Lord giveth and the Lord taketh. It is not our place to say when it is our time."

Mamas words of wisdom always stuck with me. She was a valiant woman and lived her life like a trooper. She weathered every storm and sheltered us as much as she could from pain. She lived her life for the sake of her children and everyone, knew that. She was called, Mother Jones and rightfully so. Her tenderness spread to everyone and reached those in need. Mom's place was like God's place. That's why I know if there is a heaven she is in it. In her final hours I was privileged to touch her and to hold her hand in the fashion of a child. Nostalgic memories had come to the forefront with flashbacks of my life passing by. I shared tender moments with her. I cried silent tears. There was nothing you could hide from her. Her children were like a book whose contents was well known to her. I guess living over three quarters of a century granted one that honor. Mamas smile was like no other. She could put you at ease with the touch of her hand. When you laid your head on her shoulder she would stroke your hair and the world's problems paled. I lost my savior and hero that day of an August moon and warm sun. I can still feel the sun beaming down on me as I left the room. I departed knowing that I may never again I see my mother.

The Dream #3 (a nephew)

A fish was swimming in a tub. It was a small fish at first but kept getting bigger and bigger. Dana, my grandbaby was in the tub. The fish kept growing and growing until Dana no longer was laughing from playing with the fish, and her laughter turned into sorrows. She was beginning to sigh as the fish was wearing her out. Growing larger and larger it began jumping back and forth between two tubs, as another bathtub had emerged in the bathroom. They sat side by side with only a few feet between them. Dana was slipping further and further away but I couldn't see where she was going. It seemed that she was shrinking more and more and disappearing in the water. Her small size was diminished next to the big fish as she sank under the surface. The splashing continued and became more forceful. It was as if the fish was enjoying thrusting its body back and forth between the tubs. My heart wept as she sank. Words rang out in my mind:

"Someone needs to get the baby! I kept saying it over and over. I asked someone if they had gotten the baby but no one replied. No one else was present in the dream –not even me. I remember the sad feeling that overwhelmed me at the end of the dream. At that point I wanted to retract everything I had seen. But I couldn't. There was no amount of rewinding that could accomplish that. Half awake, I tried to whisper to myself that it wasn't true. But the unshakable feeling of something awful was upon me once again.

I faced my fears the next morning by telling my daughter about it. She and her boyfriend were listening attentively. I also called home to see if everyone was alright. I was reluctant the most to tell my son whose daughter it was I saw in my dream. It was hard for me to tell him that I thought she was drowned by the big fish, but I did. I don't remember how he handled that. I do know that I had gotten it off my chest and the compelling sensation to do so was no longer there. Only anxiety remained – the wait and anticipation of not knowing.

That night after I had the dream I reluctantly went to sleep again. The fan was on; The one that had turned into a crow a few nights earlier. I lay there in my bed attempting to get to sleep. I must have fallen asleep. It was the middle of the night when I awoke. The black fan was staring at me. It had eyes and a hood dark hood was pulled over its head. With spooky eyes and a dark face that you couldn't see it was carrying a sheath. A long sheath that was sharp at the point. It resembled the grim reaper. I was frozen in my bed. I spoke to myself.

"Have you come to get me? Is it my turn now?"

I didn't get an answer. I truly thought I wouldn't wake up to rise out of bed that next morning. I imagined that the grim reaper was about to end my life. Maybe a heart attack or something but I certainly couldn't move from that bed. I was healthy as far as I knew so it would have been an act of God. If God had chosen to take me at that moment it would be inconvenient. I hadn't said goodbye to my children or made plans for my departure. The only thing I thought about was how fearful and all alone I was in that chilly room. No one could help me and I couldn't even scream.

Eventually the feeling passed. But as I got up and exited the room I didn't know how I could explain it. Who would believe what I just experienced. They would have thought I was crazy. I was convinced at the moment of the supernatural and unknown. I also knew how alone it felt if you were about to die. No one can save you, not anyone, if it's an act of God.

Having already felt the worst, I thought, I tried to make the best of it. Life had to go on and I was prepared that morning to go to work. Then I got the call.

My sister called me and said her son was in the hospital. She said it would take her awhile for her to get to him because she was away. She said that some family members were already with him and would keep her informed. I told her to call me back after finding out if he was okay. The next call I got from her was something I didn't want to hear. Carl was dead. He had drowned in his own fluid. The fluid had built up around his lungs and the mucous was too thick for him to breathe.

I knew right then that had been my dream.

Then one day, out of the blue, a few months later, I heard a voice. It was Carl's voice. It was as if he were in my presence but somewhat faded into the background. He told me to tell his mother that he loved her and he would be okay. He wanted her to know that he was happy and didn't want her to be sad. I drove over to her apartment to tell her. She greeted the news with somber cheer and shared it with her husband. They just stood there as if I were a messenger, and in a sense I was. I was glad that Carl had come back to me. I was glad that he was okay. I was overjoyed to know that I didn't have to worry about him after all I had been through. It brought a sense of closure. I no longer carried the guilt inside.

While in Grafenwohr, Germany, 2010

I spotted an ink spot as we were driving along the road. Everything stood out in Germany against the vast white snow. The hilly mountains were freshly laden with soft petals of snow. The land, crisp and clean, smelled like a winter sea breeze. The winding road we were traveling looked the same. I would have been lost except for the navigation of my host.

My son in law knew his way around very well. He and my daughter had been living there for a year. Their three kids were the joy of my eyes and delight of my trip.

It's amazing what a year can do when you're separated from loved ones. It can seem an eternity.

Being the trooper that he is, Josh rose to the occasion. The mission was to get me on my way to Italy to see my other daughter. She and her husband had just had a baby. I was two days shy of making the event.

I had spent Christmas with them and had a wonderful time. I had traveled thousands of miles and the time with them made it all worthwhile. I had enjoyed the time with my three grandchildren.

The lone bird that stood out was standing as if at attention at a stop sign. It was befitting for a soldier seeing how we were on base. I laughed at the thought of it – a trained bird in the army, how hilarious!

But it wasn't really hilarious when I thought about it further. I remember muttering, What a huge bird. That's got to be the biggest crow I've ever seen! My son in law peered at me as if trying to make the connection. His hands were steady on the steering wheel as we approached the stop sign. He took the road with ease as we made our way through the maze. To spy a black bird on that day and time struck me as odd. Why was that bird standing alone? And why was it there where only we could see it?

No other people were around and no other cars drove by. It was at an intersection – the base one way, the store the other. We had just left the commissary and he had taken the long way back. We didn't have time for sightseeing because my time was limited. I knew we had to hurry in order for me to catch my plane. We had a three hour drive ahead of us. The last minute stops were to make sure we had the right directions.

We left the house with my suitcase packed and ready. When Josh loaded it up it was all I could do but to say good-bye to my daughter and the kids. A tearful eye would separate us momentarily.

I had a few restless nights earlier that week and felt anxiety. I thought I had appeased it after making several phone calls back home to get in touch with family. I called my sister with the hope of reaching my son who often visited her. I was also checking on her welfare since she had recently come home from the hospital.

My daughter had arranged a cozy room for me to sleep in. I felt very comfortable to the point of wanting to move in with them. I knew this wasn't feasible however because of the little ones waiting for me back home. I had traveled clear across the ocean to a foreign land to see my little babies. Lani was Josh and Jay's newest arrival. She was one month shy of her first birthday. It was the cutest thing in the world to see the beam in her eye as she interacted with me. My motives were to spoil them while having the grandest and most memorable time possible. My daughter, being the ultimate hostess, must have had the same thing in mind for me because I didn't have to lift a finger the whole time I was there. She cooked for me every day and took me shopping. My birthday would be the next week and she surprised me by taking me out to dinner. We knew the restaurant wouldn't be crowded in the dead of winter but the food was excellent. Who would have thought that Japanese restaurant would exist in Germany. I was expecting to be served sauerkraut, German sausages, and beer.

"Mom, you are close to the army base you know, you should expect to see the same things you do in America".

I had to be reminded.

Lani was usually the one to wake me. My daughter would bring her to my room and place her in her playpen beside me. All it took was a bottle to put her back to sleep. In the next couple of hours I could expect the door to creep open ever so slightly. It would be Jo-Jo and Jer (Budda) deciding who would be the first to wake me. After a few times of the door opening and closing I would tell them to come on in. With one eye open and the other desperately wanting to be closed, I pretended to be alert.

I greeted them with cheer and happiness because there was no way of getting around it. The sound of their little puttering feet and whispering voices made me want to giggle.

Come on in boys I'd say, welcoming them with open arms. They couldn't leap far and fast enough to get on top of my bed. They soon would share the covers and snuggle as I managed a few more winks.

Lani would break the silence after a while letting everyone know she was up. Jay and Josh had already left the house so I had the kids all to myself. That was my daily ritual with them each morning until weekends.

The energy came in the house once the parents came back home. I could see that they were a cohesive and happy family. We played the game of I spy. I spy a bird I'd say to the kids as I peeked out the patio window. I spy a yellow one Jo-Jo would yell out. I spy a blue one Budda would say. Lani was simply amazed at seeing so many colorful birds flocked together. You could tell it was probably her first time to play. The bird game went on for awhile until the video games took over. With Christmas fast approaching we did a lot of shopping. So, going back and forth on base to the commissary became a ritual. Since I was there to visit family I didn't do a lot of sight- seeing. Partly because of the snow and mostly because everything was closed down because of it. Also, the Euro wasn't keeping pace with my dollar. But I had planned to spend a certain amount to make them happy at Christmas time. When Saturday came it was the parents' turn to take over their regular duties of tending to the kids. I had more time to myself and so slept in.

I can't pinpoint the day that it started but I do know what I felt. I had an uneasy feeling while going to bed one evening and remained restless. My gut feeling was that something wasn't right. I didn't have a nightmare but felt strange as if I had. The walls seemed to close in on me and I didn't feel comfortable being in the bedroom alone. There was a eerie feeling of isolation along with despair. Why or how such a cloud could come over me after having such a great time was puzzling.

The mood had been set for me that morning and I couldn't get up. I'm not afraid of monsters nor do I believe in ghosts, but I did feel the presence of something else.

I made all the phone calls later that day it was to appease my worries. I tried to shake it off. My sister said she was okay. Eventually I reached both of my sons. They were fine and so were my other children. My daughters were holding down the fort back home and taking care of the two grandbabies I left in their care.

So who was left? I didn't have an inkling who else to contact. Who else could it be? I always envision something close to home when my feelings are overwhelmed in that way.

Unable to dismiss the strangeness, I did my best to carry on.

"Mom are you okay?" my daughter asked as she stuck her head

into the room.

"I'm fine honey, I'm fine."

"Well I was just checking because you're usually up by now."

It had become late in the day and except for making the calls I had remained in bed.

I finally went downstairs to join the rest of the family. I explained to my daughter my uneasy feelings. She gave that ever so familiar response, shrugging her shoulders and mumbling, "Umm? Well maybe everything will be okay."

I felt at ease, at least temporarily.

My daughter called from Italy to give us the good news that she was in labor. Her baby girl would be born soon. I hope she makes my birthday I thought. But she didn't. She came one day late, missing it by only a few hours.

That's okay I thought, she'll still be my winter baby born in the midst of a storm just like me. How flattering.

Several days passed. My younger daughter Crystal sent me a text telling me that my grandbaby Mia missed me. She said Mia had a dream that something happened to me.

"Someone hurt grandma and cut her with a knife," she said.

Crystal didn't know about the jitteriness I had been having and the accompanying uncomfortable feelings. She only knew that I had spoken with her a few nights before asking her if she was okay.

Christmas came and went. The dream Mia had stayed with me. I had to wonder if it were me that something was supposed to happen to. I always felt that way despite my dreams proving to be otherwise.

But I hadn't had a dream this time. Only the same feelings that go along with it-the nightmare.

I found myself making another round of calls telling everyone merry Christmas. It was a cheerful time in spite of my earlier feelings.

She proceeded to tell me that they were on their way to Sacramento to visit her mother in law.

I responded that that was nice.

Martha is her spouse's mother and the grandmother to their children. Besides being close to me I think she was next runner up. Martha had moved in with my daughter and her family earlier that year. She had developed some health problems. She also wanted to move back to California to be closer to family. I could see the closeness the children had with their other grandmother. The trip to Sacramento was to insure that Martha didn't spend Christmas alone.

I hadn't heard anymore from my daughter after that and upon following up could not get a hold of her. I left several messages via voice mail and text. I even called her fiance's phone to see if they could be reached.

Days later she called me back saying Martha had died. The last thing they got to do with her was spend Christmas.

All of my feelings came to the surface: The spotting of the crow on base in the middle of winter, the uneasy sleepless few nights that I had, the crowding of space I felt with the walls sinking in, all of this was for a reason. I'd even concluded that Mia's dream had something to do with it. All warning signs of an event to follow.

Dreams usually precede a death and crows usually bring the news. But in this case something was different. I didn't have a nightmare or envision death because it wasn't my direct blood line. It took the nightmare of a child to link the two.

What I concluded from that situation was that death had been lingering around the corner and it had happened in a way similar to how Mia had dreamed about it. I also know it's never the person that you dream about but someone similar to them. In this case it was me. I am a grandma just like she. This has always been my pattern.

As sad as the days were that went by and the sorrowfulness of knowing that I wouldn't make it home in time to attend the funeral, somehow I felt connected. Another unpreventable death that was bound to happen, even if there were signs that preceded it.

My son in law drove me to the airport in Germany. That lone bird stood out in my mind. The biggest crow I had ever seen is how I would remember it. Plus the fact that it traveled all this way to give me a message. I never saw another crow after that on my entire trip. And for this one to be standing in the middle of nowhere right in front of us had been an undeniable sign.

WHEN CROWS CALL

www.ingramcontent.com/pod-product-compliance
Lightning Source LLC
LaVergne TN
LVHW011419080426
835512LV00005B/160